A Short Journey into Trauma

A Short Journey into Trauma

Understanding and Coping with Post-Traumatic Stress

Frank Parkinson

GREEN PRINT

First published in paperback in 2017
by Green Print, an imprint of
The Merlin Press Ltd
Central Books Building
Freshwater Road
London
RM8 1RX

www.merlinpress.co.uk

ISBN 978-1-85425-117-6

British Library Cataloguing in Publication Data
is available from the British Library

Printed in the UK by Imprint Digital, Exeter

Contents

Preface

ARE YOU ALL THERE?

Is the reason you picked up this book something to do with your own life experiences or are you simply interested in the subject of trauma? This book is based on some personal life experiences in the world of trauma, both civilian and military, and relates them to real events and real people and describes some of the traumatic reactions they have gone through and how they might be helped. It also looks at the historical background to treatment and at what treatments might be offered to those who suffer and shows that human existence is sometimes exciting, stimulating and enjoyable but can also be precarious, destructive and extremely distressing. Past events and experiences, whether traumatic or not, can influence our lives forever. The fact is that we all experience trauma of one kind or another at different times in our lives. I have frequently heard someone say, 'I've never experienced anything traumatic in my life', and, when they do, I always ask them, "I suppose you were born?" The very act of being born is traumatic for both the mother and baby and learning to cope with the many changes we experience as we grow up leads to some experiences of trauma and loss. In order to cope with this loss we have to adapt and move on. The pattern is:

Growth–Change–Loss–Adapting–Coping

Trying to cope with any changes might mean that we use positive coping strategies and find it easy to adapt but, if the strategies we use don't work and make matters worse, we can suffer from a variety of physical and emotional changes and reactions which can harm or even destroy our lives. Of course, loss can be positive or negative: going to school for the first time can be either traumatic, when we become distressed and cry, or exciting as we face new people and new challenges. Moving into a new relationship or into a new job are forms of loss because we have to change and adapt our lives in order to cope, but, hopefully, these will be positive and enjoyable experiences. Having a baby is a loss: a loss of freedom to do exactly what you wish when you want to because there is another person's welfare to consider. But, again, hopefully this is a positive loss. This pattern of growth, change, loss, adapting and coping happens constantly throughout our lives as we continue to attempt to cope with life and living. Sometimes the result is that we just can't cope with what's happening and we move into distress, confusion, depression and anxiety and react with frustration and anger and, sometimes, something more disturbing: we feel that there must be something seriously wrong with us. We have failed in some way and might even think that we are being punished for something we have done or, worst of all, are going mad. "Why can't I cope? What's wrong with me?"

Many years ago, an elderly vicar was asked by a friend, the chaplain of a large psychiatric hospital who was going on holiday, to take a service in the hospital chapel. The old vicar had no experience of such hospitals but decided that in his sermon he would preach about the meaning of life. The chapel was packed with patients and a few members of staff. He climbed into the huge pulpit, leaned forward and in a loud, piercing voice cried, "Why are we here?" There was a deathly silence until a tiny voice piped up from the back of the chapel, "Because we're not all there!"

This story might not be quite politically correct but it makes an important comment about human life and our natural and normal human feelings. In fact we are all 'not all there', but we are here and we are human! The human condition can be one of striving to do what we believe to be best, getting on with our lives and coping, but finding that life can sometimes turn our lives upside down. We question the meaning, fairness and purpose of life and our own existence.

People who are traumatised can feel that they are 'not all there' but it is important that such feelings and emotions, during and after traumatic experiences, are seen as natural and normal reactions. However, when we look at post-traumatic stress disorder we will see that this is a condition which can destroy relationships and lives and it is not sufficient to say, "Don't worry! Your reactions are natural and normal!" Perhaps this book will give some pointers as well as information and even some comfort in knowing that you are not alone. Although to a large extent our life experiences do determine who and what we are, we can challenge them and, hopefully, from our own resources, or sometimes with the help of others, learn to cope. We are not just programmable robots: we can learn to cope.

We will look at various experiences of trauma: how children react to trauma and the need for them to be given understanding and help; civilian experiences of disaster and other traumatic events and incidents; experience of war and combat and especially at how attitudes to people with psychological problems have changed dramatically over the years. There have always been the 'unbelievers' who say that there is no such thing as stress and trauma, except for the weak. We will challenge such attitudes, giving examples from history, from the ancient Greek wars, the American Civil War, the First and Second World Wars, to the conflicts of the present day. There are also many ideas and theories about why some suffer while others seem to cope and this will lead us to look at and understand how and why reactions might develop and the techniques and treatments for helping those who suffer from post-traumatic stress and post-traumatic stress disorder. We will look at examples from major disasters such as the Rwanda crisis, the bombing of the US Embassy in Nairobi, experience of aid-agency work and from war and combat, and the effects of cumulative and long-term stress. We shall also examine the strategies used by professionals and members of the emergency services to cope with traumatic events. There are examples from individuals whose lives have been damaged or devastated by their personal experiences of trauma: from traffic accidents, being held hostage, rape, armed robberies and other events. If you are suffering, or know of someone who is, at the end of the book there are lists of books and of organisations that you can contact for advice and help.

Because of the nature of some of the events described, I have changed names of people and places to protect confidentiality. I thank Relate, the organisation which trained me in counselling, and the 'Swindon Trauma Group' for their support and friendship and I also thank the Chaplain General of the Prison Service for allowing me to include material about the prison riots in Manchester. I also remember and thank all those whose lives have collided with mine over the years and who have taught me much both about life and the nature of trauma, as well as those whose lives have been shattered or maimed by traumatic events. I never fail to be comforted by the resilience and strength found in some whose experiences can make others feel so inadequate but who can be an inspiration to the human desire to live a full, happy and meaningful life, not in spite of what the world has thrown at them, but because of it.

Throughout the book I will be referring to post-traumatic stress (PTS), and post-traumatic stress disorder (PTSD), which are described in detail in Chapter 4.

The background

Thinking about and writing this book has made me more aware and certain that my life seems to have been a succession of traumatic experiences, albeit some years apart, and mostly the traumas of other people, but are experiences which have guided my life. I decided to write the book including personal experiences but didn't want it to be like Narcissus, gazing into the water and falling in love with his own reflection! But I must make one important comment.

In 1982 I was posted as Chaplain to the Royal Military College of Science, now the Defence Academy of the UK, at Shrivenham, ten miles east of Swindon, near to where I live. I had been there about four months when a young wife came to speak to me over coffee after the morning service. 'Padre', she said, 'I would just like to thank you for your services. I really do enjoy them.' I preened a little and thanked her for her kind words. It's always good to receive compliments. 'Yes', she said, 'and I really enjoy your sermons. In fact, I can understand every word you say.' I thanked her again. 'You know', she said, 'When your predecessor was here, when he preached, I couldn't understand a word he said.' There was a long pause, then she added, 'But then … he was very clever!'

Balloon deflated: but I hope I know what she meant.

So, this will not be a complicated book using lots of professional jargon but will be fairly straightforward because I also like to know what I am talking or writing about. Also, it will be presented largely in chronological order of when the events occurred. With this in mind, I begin with what was the most formative experience of trauma in my life.

Chapter I

INTRODUCTION TO TRAUMA

Some people have vivid memories of their childhood and early life but I can remember very little except for one ongoing traumatic experience that has affected my life to this day. It began in the autumn of 1945.

I don't remember much about the Second World War, except the gas masks we were given, and I remember hiding under the stairs when the air-raid warnings sounded and going with other schoolchildren to see the wreckage of a Heinkel 111 bomber which had crashed near Durham City. But the most traumatic event began in 1945 when my father returned from the war. I can vaguely remember seeing him, I think, only twice during the war. He was a military policeman and had gone to France on D-Day. But I do remember his home-coming, bringing with him a German Iron Cross and other medals, a German officer's cap and some toys he had picked up in Belgium and Germany. I was eight years old and confused by the presence of this strange and unfamiliar man. Who was he and what was he doing here?

Like millions of others, my father returned to a world which was unfamiliar: his home and business had been taken over by a group of people who had learned to cope without him. He was confronted by a closed circle of women who ran everything: my mother, his mother, my mother's mother, his sister and a woman friend who came every day to help in the house. When we moved into Durham city shortly after the war ended, my mother's cousin, a young woman, also came to live with us. At a later stage, when my father became a farmer, a large elderly aunt, who had a wooden leg, also came to stay and my mother's mother came to live in a cottage minutes away from the farm. My father was surrounded constantly in the house by three, and sometimes four, women. I do believe that it was difficult, if not impossible, for him to 'get back into the family' and I know that this was a common experience for many men, women and families after the war or, in fact, after any war or long absence of a parent or partner. Years later, my father told me that he and many other soldiers, before they were demobbed, were told to go home and not talk about their experiences, because people at home had endured their own deprivations, problems and fears and wouldn't understand anyway. It took me many years into my adult life to understand what it must have been like for him when he returned home, and the impact and significance of this, but I believe that he existed on the periphery of the family. He was an outsider and I believe that his reactions were largely the result of this.

One response was that he began to talk in great detail about his own childhood and his father, but especially he talked about his war experiences at every opportunity. If you said, 'Dad, look at that lovely tree over there', a typical reply would be to tell you, and anyone nearby, about an exciting or humorous incident in which he was involved during the war. He would tell us what the weather was like, where he was at the time, the names of those with him and details about what happened. They were very long stories! You might remember 'Uncle Albert', the old bearded sailor from the TV series 'Only Fools and Horses' who had been in the Second World War, who would say, 'During the war ...' and everyone would walk away, or Del Boy and Rodney would tell him to keep quiet. My father was like 'Uncle Albert', only worse! So, I was brought up from my early years in a family where the war was very real and very much still alive, not only for him, but for all the family. His stories were never conversations where you could make comments or ask questions: once the story started it would just go on and on and on without a pause. Also, it was obvious from his stories that he was a fully paid-up member of the 'Stiff Upper-lip Club'. Another response, and much more influential than his stories, was his extreme anger and frustration, which he expressed verbally and physically in ways that I won't describe, except for one event.

When I had my first book, *Post Trauma Stress*, published in 1993, after I left the army, I sent him a copy and later, when visiting my parents, I asked my father what he thought of the book. He said that it was all very interesting but that 'we didn't have any of that psychological "clap-trap" in the army but just had to get on with it'. I then asked him why he talked so much about the war. His reply was, "You young people (I was fifty-six at the time) don't know what war is like. It was the most important experience of my life!" We were on our own in the room so I said that he talked about incidents which were largely humorous, such as the day he chased a pig around a field and had pork for supper, but that he had never spoken about anything awful or traumatic. His stories were always humorous or exciting and he would always tell them with great relish. Because we were on our own, I asked him if he had ever done anything which had been difficult or traumatic and if he had ever seen anybody killed. There was a long pause. He stared at me, tears came into his eyes and he began to cry. Gradually he told me about an incident where some men he knew had been killed by shell-fire and he and some colleagues had gone to help with the bodies. This was a difficult moment for both of us because I had never seen him cry before and he was finding it difficult to talk, but he quickly recovered and just sat there in silence, staring at me. A few minutes later I went into the kitchen where my mother was working but, unknown to me or my father, she had been listening to our conversation. She was astonished and said, 'I've been married to your father for nearly sixty years and he has never told me that!'

I don't believe that my father had PTSD but am certain that he suffered from post-traumatic stress. I am convinced that talking about his childhood, his father and the war, were ways of trying to cope with his memories and re-establish his identity and importance within the family. But it didn't work out like that. What I do believe is that in addition to his war experiences, some of which were traumatic, he had lost his status as a father and head of the family. He was an 'outsider' and, as he grew older, he became more and more distant, isolated and verbally and physically angry.

I believe that being brought up in an atmosphere which centred on the Second World War, and living with a remote and very angry father, has influenced my life to this day and partly determined some of my life choices. It certainly influenced my childhood and upbringing. Is this why I chose to be a clergyman, to join the army, train as a counsellor and to work for many years in the field of trauma? Incidentally, one of my sons is a qualified psychiatric nurse! Have my life choices influenced him?

❖ Children and trauma

The poet William Wordsworth wrote that 'the child is father of the man', so it is important to understand how children might react to traumatic events, events which might affect them throughout their lives. Looking at childhood experiences and memories can also help us to understand how these have affected us and helped to make us what we are as adults. So how do children react to traumatic experiences? Some will cope well and enjoy changes and it is easy to assume that they are not affected, but they can react, sometimes later, in unexpected and dramatic ways.

Children can react to traumatic events, including bereavement, in similar ways to adults, but they usually handle and cope with them differently. How they do this will be determined partly by their age, upbringing and level of development. Until a certain age, which varies with each child, they might not have the language and vocabulary that enables them to say what they think or feel. Reactions can happen before, during or following any event which might disturb or distress them: losing a family member, pet or a friend; being taken into care or being told that they were adopted; experiencing parental separation and divorce; being bullied or sexually and physically abused; moving home or school or being sent to a 'prep' or public school; the illness of a family member. Any of these, and similar experiences, can result in disruptive play, fear, anxiety, self-blame and guilt.

Some will act out of character and become surly or aggressive and uncooperative, especially in the way they play their games, either on their own or with others. They might invent or find new games, especially those involving violence and aggressive behaviour such as playing soldiers or war games or acting out situations where there is distress or violence.

One four-year-old boy had been involved in a hostage situation in Iraq and had been released, but his father was still being held and in danger. He was playing with Lego pieces and had made a figure of a man with four small white blocks attached to the top of his head which he said was a man who had been hurt and the blocks were bandages! Could it have been his 'daddy' and was he showing something of his inner anxiety in this way?

Children can be aggressive with parents, friends or other children both at home, at play and in school and destroy toys and playthings and become demanding, disruptive and destructive. Some children will retreat into their own world, becoming quiet and uncommunicative, lose their appetite, play on their own and shun contact with their siblings and friends, and they might also reject parental affection. Some children will express their feelings through drawings and paintings.

A little girl of eight years, whose father was away in the first Gulf War, had drawn her own picture of what she said was 'daddy as a soldier'. She put this drawing on her bedside locker next to his photograph and told her mother that she would only take her drawing away, "when daddy comes home".

Perhaps she was acting out her anxiety and worry about her father in this way by having her own drawing next to his photograph, symbolising her concern that he might not come home. There are psychologists and therapists specialising in art and play therapy with children who use dolls and toys and encourage them to play and draw or paint. These drawings and paintings can often tell something about the hidden fears, anxieties and concerns of the child.

Children can be afraid of almost any changes taking place in their lives, and they may react not only during and after an event, but also before it. Moving home can be exciting but means leaving and losing a familiar family house and home, friends and neighbours, a school and various social activities and having to adjust and adapt. Also, children usually have no control over what happens in their lives and this can make any changes more threatening and disturbing. Where there are traumatic incidents and experiences children can react by being frightened, even of going to bed. A young child was told, when his grandfather died, that, "Grandpa has gone to sleep", and he became terrified of going to bed at night. He thought that if he went to sleep he would become like his grandfather and die.

Partly because they have no control over events, children can blame themselves for changes which take place in their lives. Problems between parents can be internalised and children might believe that they are to blame for their parents' problems, separation or divorce or even their illnesses. In cases of child physical abuse, including sexual abuse, it is common for a child to believe that it is their fault and this feeling can persist into and affect adult life. Parents and other adults can seem like giants or gods who are always right and the reaction from a child can be (and it might not be 'Daddy' but someone else): 'Daddy only treats me like this because I am bad.'

It is particularly terrible for children to believe not just that they are unloved but to believe that they are unlovable and that 'nobody could love me!' This feeling of being 'unlovable' can continue into an adult's life until the day they die and affect self-esteem and the ability to form good and positive relationships.

Anxiety can be shown through extra sensitivity to any criticism. Some children might need or seek extra affection, demanding or needing more hugs and cuddles and closeness to a parent and might need more reassurance that they are still loved and loveable. Some will accept this extra love and affection but others might reject any offers of physical contact or comfort, much to the hurt and misunderstanding of parents, teachers, family or friends.

Children might complain of minor illnesses and problems: tummy-aches, headaches, and various other pains: feeling tired and listless and not wanting to do anything or go anywhere; an inability to relax or sleep; not wanting to go to school or to play with friends. Older children might return to an old teddy bear or toy or to sucking a thumb: to something they found comforting when younger. They might also return to a previous childhood pattern of behaviour such as being clinging or needy, having temper tantrums, crying or even wetting the bed and having bad dreams and nightmares.

A mother had been involved in an armed robbery in the building society where she worked. Nobody had been hurt physically, but her young children became anxious and tearful and very clinging. They did not want her to go to work or even leave the house. One morning, when she was getting ready for work, her little girl, age six, asked her anxiously and with tears in her eyes, 'Mummy, will you be coming home again tonight?'

It is a common misconception that children are not affected by changes in their lives and will cope well with bereavement, grief and loss, and they are often ignored following traumatic events or experiences. Adults might be offered help through counselling, or even just sympathy from others and a listening ear, but the children's needs might not even be considered. For all children, loss is an integral part of their experience, from loss of the security of the womb to many other changes which take place both to them and to their surroundings. Some will try to protect their children from such events in the belief that they will not understand and might be upset. Seeing parents grieving can be distressing for children but if it is explained to them why their parents are crying and upset it can be part of their preparation for life. Those involved, especially in helping roles, should not forget the possible reactions and needs of any children. They will need, reassurance, security, comfort and love and a great deal of care and understanding. As with adult reactions to traumatic events, the reactions of children should usually be seen as natural and normal under the circumstances and not signs of delinquency or deviance. Children can also develop symptoms of PTSD, and this is described and discussed in Chapter 4.

Chapter 2

LEARNING ABOUT TRAUMA

In 1995, at the age of eighteen, I was called-up to do National Service in the Royal Air Force. At one stage I was posted to a station where an aircraft had recently crashed nearby and the pilot was burned to death.

I noticed that the station RAF firemen had a very strange way of greeting each other. When they met, one would say to the other, 'Hello! Fred!' and would then crouch half down, gurn up his face with a rictus grin, make a groaning sound and hold up both hands with his fingers tightly curled. The other would reply in the same manner. I asked one of the firemen why they did this strange greeting. 'What greeting?' he asked, so I demonstrated it. 'Oh!' he said, "That's how the body looked in the cockpit".

At the age of eighteen and wet behind the ears, I thought this was awful but later realised that sick-humour can be a useful coping strategy – as long as it is not used all the time!

❖ The traumas of parish life

In 1962 I was ordained into the Church of England and went to serve a curacy in a parish. At that time people who had served in the Second World War could be as young as thirty-five so there were many young men and women around who had vivid and personal memories of the war. My experience was that most people never spoke about it, except for my father!

The vicar of the parish had been an army chaplain during the war, was captured in 1940, just before Dunkirk, and put into a prisoner of war camp. Eventually, as a non-combatant, he was offered repatriation but refused because he said that he wanted to stay with his men. He mentioned his military experience to me only once, when he knew that I was to join the army, and that was to say how difficult a time he had as a prisoner of war: but he gave no details. His reputation in the diocese was as a dedicated and energetic priest and, while he did live up to his reputation, he was, in some ways, a physical and nervous wreck. He suffered almost constantly from eczema and shingles and would frequently be scratching away at his hands, chest and head. The most difficult thing for his staff was that he communicated with us largely by note. We would go into the church every morning to say our prayers together and find a piece of paper on our prayer desks telling us what to do that day or over the next few days. He didn't speak to us very often but seemed to live in a little enclosed world and we were never invited into the vicarage except for the very occasional staff meeting. I now believe that he was suffering from a form of post-traumatic stress, but such terms were not used at the time. He had certainly been badly affected by his imprisonment and experience of the war, and it showed. In spite of this, or maybe because of it, he was a wonderful character and well-loved priest.

In the same parish I bought a small car and went to the local petrol station for the first time. A man in his late thirties came to fill up my car, put the nozzle into the petrol tank and his right foot onto the rear bumper. I noticed that there was a livid scar around his ankle and said that this looked quite nasty and asked him how he got it. He looked at me and said, 'that's where they chained me to a wall in Changi camp'. He was captured in the Far East and became a prisoner of war with the Japanese. I asked him what it had been like and he began to talk, and talk, and talk! Almost an hour later when I left the station I realised that all I had done was listen and occasionally nod my head. Every time I called for petrol he would continue to tell me, and at great length, about his experiences and I knew that if I needed petrol I had to make sure that I had plenty of time to listen. At that time I knew nothing much about helping people who had experienced trauma other than as a result of bereavement and personal, marital or family problems and I did nothing more than listen. I don't know if this helped him or not, but he certainly needed to talk.

In 1964 I moved to a parish in Liverpool during which time I became a chaplain in the Territorial Army and enjoyed this 'part-time soldiering' so much that in 1967 I joined the regular army as a Chaplain.

❖ Army chaplain 1967-1992

From my experience as a chaplain I came to believe that the negative attitudes towards welfare problems held by many people in the armed services that I encountered, including reactions to stress and post-traumatic stress, were due to a general 'macho' view of life. I knew that these attitudes were mirrored in other organisations in the civilian world and in society in general: 'Men should not, and do not, suffer from stress or reactions to traumatic events and, if you have problems, you are not a real man: just get over it!' There was also the belief that individuals and families should not have problems and, if they did, it was because they were inadequate and pathetic. Looking at how welfare and trauma, counselling and helping, were viewed by many in the army can help us understand the same attitudes experienced in civilian life. The following story is one example of a general, negative and unhelpful attitude, even from professionals.

In the late 1960s I was stationed in Germany and visiting a military hospital maternity ward where a young wife I knew had just had her first baby. I asked permission from the ward sister to see her and walked into the single room where I found her sitting up in bed with a brilliant smile on her face. I looked for the baby. There was no cot in the room. My gut began to feel that something was seriously wrong. We talked for a few minutes and, feeling increasingly anxious, I asked her about the baby. She smiled and said, 'It's all right. The sister has said that they have buried her in the rose-garden. We just have to put it behind us, wait a few months and try again.' I thought that perhaps she was in a state of shock and denial and that she might be confused and wrong about what had happened so I went to see the ward sister and asked about the baby. At first she was reluctant to say anything, but then she told me that the baby had been stillborn. When I queried the burial in the rose garden she immediately became defensive and said, very aggressively, 'Well, that's what we tell them'. I knew then that the dead baby had been burnt in the hospital incinerator and said so but the nurse refused to acknowledge it. The advice on having a stillborn baby was to forget the problem, just get on with it and try again! So much for compassionate attitudes to bereavement and trauma! I contacted the military authorities and, eventually, was told that this would never happen again in any military hospital.

While stationed in Germany I visited Northern Ireland a num-ber of times and became aware of the possible psychological and physical effects of deployment on soldiers and also on their families left behind. In our army schools teachers said that it was easy to spot the children whose fathers were away on deployment by their behaviour. As has already been emphasised, there is still a misconception that children are too young to be affected by loss and trauma. However, there is some evidence to show that the children, and even grandchildren of Holocaust survivors, can develop symptoms of PTS, or even PTSD by repeatedly hearing the dreadful accounts of the horrors of the concentration camps: a kind of 'traumatic reaction by association'. The needs of children should never be ignored, but their distress might not be acknowledged, or understood, even by professionals. A similar experience happened much later, in 1982, when I was stationed in the UK.

My twelve-year-old son brought a fellow student home from the local school. His parents had separated and he was living with his mother and her new partner. He was extremely upset, distressed and traumatised, not only by the breakup of his parents' relationship but also because his mother's new partner had physically assaulted him a number of times. He came to stay with us and we reported the assaults to the police and social services. Two police officers arrived and saw the bruises but they said that there was no point in taking this further because it would get nowhere in court and be too distressing for all concerned. They wouldn't even go to see his mother or her partner. A few days later, a social worker arrived and she too saw the bruises. Her advice was that the boy should do nothing because it might harm the 'primary relationship' between the woman and her partner. I couldn't believe it! The mother was still claiming child-allowance but didn't even want to see him. Eventually we discovered that the boy had a grandmother in London and he went to live with her. The boy was not offered any help, support or counselling and the police officers and Social Worker didn't even ask him what had happened, how he was feeling, where he was going to live or how he was coping. Their main concern was not the boy's welfare but the welfare of those causing the trauma. Again, this attitude was not just peculiar to these 'professionals' but the result of a more general attitude in society to traumatic experiences which said, 'forget it, put it behind you and get on with your life!'

❖ Counselling training, welfare and trauma

In 1982 I applied for training with Relate, a nationwide counselling agency, was accepted and began training which took place over the next two and a half years. This was the best thing I had ever done professionally. In 1960, as a student, I had to attend a series of lectures by a psychiatrist at Liverpool University and I recall that he said, "When you see a roaring lion of a person, look for a little frightened mouse hiding inside. When you see a little frightened mouse of a person, look for a roaring lion waiting to get out". This sounds very simple but there is an element of truth in it because it has sometimes helped me to understand myself and other people. Looking at this counselling training can help us to understand more about helping those suffering from traumatic stress.

In the 1980s, Relate training was in what is called the 'psychodynamic mode' which, simply put, looks at the ways in which life experiences from childhood to the present, and what is happening now, can influence and affect our lives. Understanding who and what we have been can determine who we are now and give us some clues as to how and why we react to life events in the present. This can help us not only to understand ourselves but also help us to know what is possible for us. At that time, Relate training used a three stage model known as the Carkhuff-Egan Model, a model also reflected in the way therapists treat those suffering from PTS and PTSD. This will be discussed in Chapter 6.

The Carkhuff-Egan model

The basis of this model is similar to the natural response we might make to someone who is distressed where we would tend to ask certain questions showing our willingness to listen and to help. For example:

If you met with a friend and noticed that she looked worried, what would you do? Probably the first thing would be to ask her if she is all right. 'I'm OK,' is her response. You might then say, 'come and sit down and I'll get some coffee'. You get the coffee, sit down and ask, 'You look a bit anxious and worried. Is something wrong?' After a pause, she replies, 'Well, I feel upset, humiliated and angry. Something has happened and I don't know what to do.' You then ask if she would like to talk about it and she begins to tell you her story. You listen carefully, sometimes asking a question and being genuinely interested in what she has to say. Eventually she asks you, 'Yes! It's all right talking, but what can I do about it?' You might then begin to help her to look at what is possible for her, what help might be available and you offer your support.

This is similar to the three-stage 'Carkhuff-Egan' model of 'exploration, understanding and action'.

• **Exploration stage**: what has happened and what is happening now. This includes looking at as many aspects of their life now as they feel able to talk about or recall.

• **Understanding stage**: you help to create understanding and this stage provides a link to the next stage and is based on the belief that: "If I can understand what is happening now, why it might be happening, where I have come from and what experiences I have had in the past, then perhaps this can throw some light on my life and problems now and help me to make decisions as to what I can do about them."

• **Action stage**: help people to look at the possible choices they have and what might be the consequences of any choices? What are their limitations, aspirations and needs and what information might help them in trying to resolve the problems?

This three-stage model is reflected in most of the various models, described later in Chapter 6 and Chapter 8, of helping after a traumatic experience: what have you experienced, how has it affected you and what can be done about it?

❖ Army welfare and trauma

From the early 1980s, my involvement in attempting to influence attitudes within the army towards welfare and trauma was because I believed that certain attitudes and the system itself should be changed. There was a genuine concern, caring and support in regiments and units for those with problems, but some attitudes were inappropriate and based on mistaken beliefs and prejudices. From the early 1980s, and my involvement in army courses on welfare at Bristol University, it was evident that there was a great deal of misunderstanding about the nature of personal and family problems as well as resistance to accepting that traumatic reactions were not signs of weakness or inadequacy. Even in the 1990s, the masculine, 'macho' attitude was still very evident and very strong. However, attitudes did begin to change and, in the later years of my involvement in the courses, some welfare officers were able to talk, not only about welfare problems and the realities of stress and trauma, but also about their own personal experiences and difficulties. In spite of this, there was, and still is, a need to change attitudes to trauma, not only in the army but also in society.

In 1982, while on a course at St George's House, Windsor, I wrote a 'paper' about welfare in the army and suggested that there should be two major changes: changes in attitudes and changes in the system and organisation of welfare.

• Changes in attitudes

When I joined the army in 1967 a sergeant told me, probably with tongue in cheek, that the army system of welfare used what was called the Sunshine Method. When I asked what this was he said:

> Well, Padre, if someone comes to you and says, for example, that he is having problems in his marriage and his wife is threatening to leave him, you grab him by the throat and say, 'Now, look here, sunshine! Get yourself sorted out and come back tomorrow with the solution or you're posted'. That's the Sunshine Method!

This was, of course, a caricature of the welfare system as it was then, but there was an element of truth in it. Welfare in the army was, and still is, based on the belief that 'welfare is a function of command' – that those in authority, at every level, have the responsibility of caring for and helping people with problems. However, some believed that people with problems were actually 'problem people', and problem people didn't deserve help and should not be in the army. Some, even amongst those in authority, believed that there was no such thing as psychological trauma, except for those who were weak-willed and beyond contempt. A common response when discussing trauma was: 'Problem people are people the army can do without, so, get rid of them.' However, I believed that without a move from old, dismissive, authoritarian and paternalistic attitudes, soldiers and families would suffer. Such attitudes take us back to the First World War and the belief that those who suffered from 'shell-shock' and 'nerves' were undeserving cowards who should not be helped, but removed, or, if they were unlucky, shot!

Like some others, I believed that the answer to the problem of unhelpful attitudes to welfare was that those specifically involved in welfare, should be specially selected and receive professional training. This included a better understanding of personal and social problems such as bereavement and marital breakdown and eventually, Post-Traumatic-Stress-Disorder. This began to happen.

• Changes in the system

As well as the belief and practice in units that 'welfare is a function of command', there was no shortage of people who could help: medical personnel, chaplains, unit welfare officers, the Army Welfare Service and civilian helpers, but there was a tendency for some personnel to work alone and to keep problems 'in-house'. Sometimes this worked well but, when attempts to help are unsuccessful, the result can be frustration, anger and a sense of failure for both helper and client. Where appropriate and necessary, those involved in welfare should work with each other and also liaise with local civilian professionals. Today, attitudes have changed for the better and those involved in welfare in the army are now more professionally trained and the system and organisation has improved, but in 1985 there were still 'unbelievers', even amongst chaplains!

Some chaplains, fortunately only a few, did not understand why I was training in counselling. A senior chaplain app-roached me at a conference in 1985 and said, 'What's this counselling thing you are doing?' I said that it was the best thing I had ever done professionally and started to tell him about it. He interrupted and said, 'I don't need any of that counselling nonsense. When I go into any situation I take with me two thousand years of Christian spirituality'. I said, 'I haven't a clue what you are talking about'. He walked away in a huff! Strange, that some of those who, as part of their work, will often be close to people in their deepest need or suffering, including those with symptoms of stress, PTS or PTSD, should believe that empathy, understanding, compassion and the ability to be a good listener, helper and counsellor are not useful skills to have and should not be part of our remit. For this senior chaplain, perhaps these qualities, suddenly came down from Heaven when, at ordination, the bishop laid hands on his head! Such is life!

• Leaving the armed services

In the armed services, personnel suffering from traumatic stress, especially PTSD, were usually discharged and then became the responsibility of the NHS and, unfortunately, also of the sparse availability in civilian life of resources for help and support. Those who are discharged with psychological problems, in spite of the existence of many civilian charities, organisations and government initiatives, can find it very difficult to look for, ask for or find help. In cases of traumatic-stress reactions there is also the anxiety, stigma, social withdrawal, disorientation, frustration, and shame attached to having problems and these can deter people from admitting that they need help. Asking for help can be seen as a sign of weakness with the belief that 'nobody can help and no one can understand'.

This can also apply, perhaps to a lesser degree, to those who leave the armed services because of retirement, redundancy, injury or illness. Leaving the armed services can be quite a shock, because each has its own particular culture and way of life and those leaving can suddenly find that they are thrust out of that family into what they can experience as a strange and alien world where most civilians do not understand the nature, humour, camaraderie, discipline, danger, excitement, fear and safety of military life. Those who leave the armed services should not, as one suffering, discharged soldier said, 'be put onto the scrapheap of society where nobody understands or cares'. Those who have served in a closely knit unit, especially during and after combat, can experience a fellowship and comradeship which creates relationships closer than loving a partner. One group especially at risk are 'reservists', who can do a six month tour of duty and then return to civilian life where they do not have the support available to full-time armed services' personnel where the ship, unit, regiment squadron or station is their 'family'.

❖ Beyond endurance

In 1986 I came across a book which began to change my way of thinking about trauma. Beyond Endurance by Glin Bennet, a consultant psychiatrist and psychotherapist at Bristol University, is a book about pilots, sailors, soldiers, train drivers, victims of terrorism, torture, disaster, mountain climbers and adventurers of all kinds who have been pushed beyond their physical and psychological limits. It also describes ways in which some people respond to traumatic experiences. Partly as the result of reading Glin Bennet's book, and discovering more about extremely stressful situations and their effect on people, I was encouraged to discover and read more about trauma and to find out as much as I could about PTS and PTSD. Some experiences of trauma are difficult to believe.

❖ Things that go bump in the night!

I have had experience in the army of a number of incidents which did not result in post-traumatic stress disorder but certainly resulted in trauma and PTS where the people involved were terrified and anxious to the extent that it severely affected what they were thinking and how they were feeling and living.

• When Murphy went mad in the NAAFI – 1969

I was stationed in Germany at the time of this event. One evening, around 10.00 p.m., my home telephone rang. It was a sergeant major from the local regiment who said, 'Padre! You'd better come quickly. Murphy has gone mad in the NAAFI'. I duly went to the NAAFI, which was a very large room upstairs in an old barrack-block building. For those who do not know, the NAAFI, the 'Navy, Army and Air Force Institutes', provided a supermarket-type store as well as a bar and a recreation place for soldiers. A large number of soldiers were milling around on the steps and in the entrance to the building. I walked into the room where I saw Murphy on the floor being held down by six soldiers. He was screaming, shaking and fighting like an animal. I went and stood at Murphy's feet, so that he could see me and my dog-collar. He immediately stopped fighting and shaking, looked at me and started to cry. I told the soldiers to help him to his feet and leave him alone. Murphy walked towards me, threw his arms around me and began to sob. I told the sergeant major to clear the room and steps and call for the medical officer, who I assumed would arrive within a few minutes. The sergeant major left the room and I was then alone with Murphy. The sergeant major was standing at the door. I took Murphy to an armchair and sat directly opposite him. He was breathing normally and able to talk so, eventually, I asked him about his background and family. He came from a large Roman Catholic family in Eire where he was very strictly brought up in a small village. He explained that he was very religious and that his mother had instilled in him a belief in the 'banshee' which he said was a wailing, evil spirit usually foretelling death. He said he believed that this evil spirit was possessing him and holding him in its grip. He was sitting quietly and talking, looking straight at me but, as he talked, he gradually began to change. His face became grim, his eyes widened, his breathing became rapid and he began to groan and growl and grind his teeth. He would then go back to being almost normal and begin to talk but would then say 'It's coming back' and that this evil spirit was returning. He then acted in this frightening manner as the spirit came back and went away and that's how it was for about 25 minutes! When this reaction happened he gripped my hands very tightly, hurting me. Each time, I looked directly at him, made the sign of the cross and told him that all was well and that he would be all right and this calmed him down. Eventually the medical officer, a friend and colleague, who looked rather like Eric Morecambe, arrived and we took Murphy to the medical centre. Eventually, Murphy returned to the UK for treatment and then left the army.

Throughout this event, I was absolutely terrified, not by any evil spirit, which I did not believe in anyway, but the fact that Murphy was a huge and muscular man who could quite easily have injured me. As far as I know, Murphy was not drunk or on drugs but I believed that he was having some major psychological disturbance and reaction. Even though Murphy was now under medical care and I was safe, I still had some sleepless nights and it did disturb me for some time after. As I write this, I can begin to feel some of the fear I felt then, but it is just a very slight memory. At the time, I certainly had a mild form of PTS.

• Dracula's curse – 1976

While stationed in Cyprus, a young soldier and his wife, Mark and Barbara, asked me to baptise their baby, so I called one evening to discuss the service and to complete the necessary forms. As we talked, I had a feeling that there was something wrong so asked them if they were worried about anything. They looked at each other and said, "Shall we tell him?" They told me that the young couple living opposite, Jenny and Tom, also wanted their baby baptised but were too frightened to ask me. When I asked why this was they suggested that we go to see them, which we did. With two sleeping babies in the room, we all sat around ready to talk. Jenny, who was breathing very heavily and quickly, was shaking and looked terrified, said that she and her family were under the control of Count Dracula. They were too frightened to go out at night and didn't know what to do because she knew that

Dracula was waiting outside the house at night to "get me" and that she and her husband lived in perpetual fear. I asked Jenny how she knew that Dracula was real and said that he was the creation of Bram Stoker based loosely on the story of Vlad the Impaler or Vlad Dracul who fought against the Ottoman invasion in the Balkans in the fifteenth century and that Dracula meant 'Son of the Dragon' and that, apparently, he impaled enemy captives on stakes! Jenny denied this and said that she had a recording of Dracula talking, so I asked her to get it. It was an old LP which had a picture of Christopher Lee on the cover in the usual Dracula pose, teeth and all! The record cover also had information inside about Bram Stoker and Vlad Dracul but she insisted that this might be true but she just knew that Dracula was real and was there outside at night and hovering around the house. I asked her what proof she had that Dracula was really there. She said that, one evening, with her husband, Mark and Barbara, they were playing with the 'Ouija Board' so asked whether or not Dracula was real. The answer they received was that the proof would be that Jenny would find something she had lost many years ago. They suddenly heard a loud bang upstairs in their bedroom: she ran upstairs, went straight to her bedside locker drawer and found a gold ring she had lost many years ago. This was ultimate proof! I discussed the 'Ouija Board' with them but Jenny insisted that Dracula was definitely there, devastating their lives and that she was especially fearful for their baby. I said that we would have the baptism of both babies the next Sunday and that this would make Dracula go away. This we did and that's what happened. No more Dracula. About six months later I flew home to the UK on the same aeroplane as Jenny and Tom and they, and their baby, were just fine!

• The haunted bedroom – 1978

This story is also difficult to believe but it resulted in a terrified and traumatised family and their neighbours.

I was walking through the garrison in Germany when Sally, a woman vaguely familiar to me, stopped me and asked if I could help. She said that she lived in a block of flats occupied by military families and her daughter's bedroom was haunted. Everyone in the family was 'absolutely terrified and scared stiff'. I said I would call to see her and duly arrived at the flat that evening. Sally, her husband and daughter and the wife of another soldier, were all sitting bolt upright, upset, afraid and trembling and there was an atmosphere of fear and dread. I sat down and asked what had happened.

Sally said that two days ago her eight-year-old daughter had gone to bed and that she and a woman friend from a neighbouring flat were sitting drinking and talking. It was after ten o'clock when suddenly she heard a scream and her daughter came running into the room saying that there was a man in the bedroom sitting at the bottom of the bed. Sally was dismissive, but gave her daughter a hug and said that it was just a bad dream and that she would take her back to bed. As she walked into the bedroom she said that she also saw a man, sitting on the bed, was immediately in a state of shock, screamed and ran out of the room with her daughter. This also happened to her husband. They were so frightened that the other woman, who also saw the man, said that she would go and get her husband to help. A few minutes later he came barging in saying he would sort things out and went to the bedroom, but he too saw the man and was terrified and shaking with fear.

Since then they had not used the bedroom, had closed the bedroom door, were extremely frightened when passing the room, were not sleeping and were living in a state of utter terror. I asked if I could see the bedroom and Sally said that I could but shouldn't go in because it was 'terrifying and icy cold in there'. I walked into the bedroom, with Sally and the others cowering and shaking behind me, peering around the door, but, to me, the temperature felt absolutely normal. I stood silently in the room for a few minutes and then walked out and told Sally that I would sort this out: I would say a prayer and give God's blessing on the room and that all would be well. Fortunately, I had brought my clerical robes with me so got dressed up, went back into the room, with the others still trembling with fear standing outside the door, said a few prayers, asked them to join in the Lord's Prayer, and gave a blessing. And it all went away! Sally and her family said they now felt fine and went into the bedroom: no more problems! I saw Sally a few days later and she thanked me and said that everything was now 'back to normal'. I discovered later that Sally had been told some months before this event that the flats had been built after the Second World War on a site where homes had been bombed and that people had seen spirits of the dead who had been killed in the bombing!

❖ Conclusion

Whatever the cause of these three incidents, they resulted in typical reactions of PTS: persistent fear and terror, anxiety, recurring and intrusive thoughts and images, bad dreams and nightmares, feeling vulnerable and threatened, fear of darkness, palpitations, sweating and shaking, a belief that something dreadful will happen, distressing thoughts and recollections of the event and an inability to live a normal life.

There are many kinds of incidents which can traumatise people and result in the development of PTS and sometimes a firm and confident but careful approach can work wonders. Note the reaction mentioned later, from the book Band of Brothers, of an American soldier, after D-Day, who became blind but who was 'cured' by the firm but caring and confident words of his commanding officer, Richard Winters. Sadly, this is not true of all traumatic experiences.

Chapter 3

DISASTER AND WAR!

While serving in the army, I became involved with military and civilian personnel after a number of traumatic events. The following incidents are in chronological order.

- The East Midlands' air disaster – 1989

On 8 January 1989, British Midland Flight 92, a Boeing 737/400, crashed into the embankment of the M1 motorway near Kegworth in Leicestershire. Of the 118 passengers, 47 people died as a result of the crash, some at the site and others later in hospital.

On 10 January, I received a telephone call from the commanding officer of an army unit, based near Kegworth, where a number of young male and female army recruits had been taken to the site to help with the rescue and in clearing up the area. He asked me if I would go and talk to them because he knew that some had been upset by what they had seen and been asked to do. On arrival I spent some time with the senior officer discovering how these young people had been involved and what the signs were of any reactions. There were twenty people attending the sessions, both male and female. I gave a short introduction reassuring them that their reactions were normal and natural, giving examples from other traumatic events. I then split them into small mixed groups to talk about their experiences and reactions based on a number of questions. Each group had a leader and a 'scribe' to record and report findings to the large group afterwards. This seemed to go quite well and in their reports they talked about typical reactions of shock, fear, anxiety, sleeplessness and the need to suppress reactions in order to carry on. However, there was one major problem: some of the young men were wary of speaking about their work and reactions because there were young women in their group. In spite of this their reports were quite useful especially in showing some of them that they were not alone in how they were feeling and that they were not stupid or weak. I then gave a summary of their findings and spoke about the future and what they should do if their reactions continued or did not begin to reduce in intensity. As I drove home I was not altogether pleased about what I had done and thought that I could have done better: I needed a better structure. However, a few days later the commanding officer rang me and said that many of those present had said that the sessions had been helpful.

- The Manchester prison riots – 1990

On 1 April 1990 a service was taking place in the chapel of Manchester's Strangeways Prison. The chapel was full of prisoners and some civilian members of staff. There had been rumours of unrest but this was not thought to be serious. The chaplain leading the service was standing at the front holding a microphone when one of the prisoners, carrying a knife, walked out to the front, took the microphone from him and said that they were taking over the chapel and prison. The chaplain tried to calm things down but, allegedly, someone cried out, 'You've heard enough. Let's get the bastards.' Chaos then reigned. Some people left the chapel by a back door but some of the staff, clergy and teachers, were held hostage for a short while. The riots lasted for just over three weeks, until 25 April, during which parts of the prison were destroyed and the chapel was burnt down.

I was asked by the Assistant Chaplain General of the prison chaplaincy services to help the chaplaincy team and teachers who had been held hostage in the prison and were disturbed and deeply upset by what had happened. I agreed to go and then had two major tasks: to get as much information as I could about the riots and to decide what I was going to do. I contacted Janet Johnston of the Dover Counselling Centre, who was involved in the Zeebrugge disaster, and asked if she had any suggestions. I spoke about my work and background and, when I said that I was a trained counsellor, she said she would send me some information about 'psychological debriefing'. This was widely used in Scandinavia and based on the work of Dr Atlé Dyregrov, a psychologist from the University of Bergen in Norway. It involved working with groups after traumatic incidents and she encouraged me to use it. The material arrived and a group debriefing was agreed for 17–18 May with those involved. Dyregrov's model, described in detail later, was in seven stages: introduction; expectations and the facts; thoughts and sensory impressions; emotional reactions; normalisation of reactions; future planning and coping; disengagement. I decided to use this model in order to achieve the following aims:

- **To get them together** in a suitable and informal environment for a reunion where they could relax and talk and help them to see that their reactions were normal and, because they were mainly clergy, to allow them to meet for prayer and worship.
- **To give them an opportunity to talk** about what things had been like in their work before the riots broke out and to say what had happened during the riots
- **To talk about what they had felt like before, during and after the riots** and what they were feeling and thinking now.
- **To look at what resources were available** to support them now and in the future should they need help.

The venue was to be in Whalley Abbey, the Blackburn Diocesan Retreat House, a lovely old building in its own grounds in Lancashire on the southern fringes of the Lake District. Of the original Cistercian abbey, dating from 1296, only the chapel ruins remain but a large country house was built on the site in the early twentieth century. The sessions were to take place over two days with group sessions interspersed by chapel services, walks in the abbey grounds and beautiful countryside, good food, rest and relaxation and the bar in the evenings. This lovely venue was a great bonus and enabled us to meet in a relaxed atmosphere where prayer and time for thought were natural ingredients which seemed to underpin and add something to the whole process. Although some attending had not been present in the chapel on the day the riots started, they still felt the impact of the event and, as members of the chaplaincy team, wished to attend, so there were ten people present for the debriefing. Sessions were open ended but were usually one and a half to two hours long plus the fifth and final session which was described as an informal 'sharing session'.

In the two sessions, held on the first morning, we all introduced ourselves and the rules were laid down and agreed by all: no one needed to say anything if they did not wish to other than where they were at the time and what their role was; each person would be allowed their own 'space' for talking; focus should be on reactions and impressions, which were more important than seeking answers to what had happened. A brief outline of the debriefing structure was given so that they were aware of the procedure and process and everyone agreed to take part.

In the first session I asked each person to say what they had been doing and where they were before the riots broke out, especially what they felt about their work in the prison. The first reactions were of confusion and shock and talk was about how well they believed their work in the prison had been going. Main reactions were of anger, annoyance, fear and frustration with a sense of unreality in an atmosphere of total disbelief that this could be happening. It should not have happened: it was like a bad dream or nightmare. One important fact emerged early on: the prison was seen not just as a building and place of work but more like a large family home and that the destruction of the prison and, more especially for them, burning down the chapel, was the destruction of a whole community and way of life. Some spoke of the prison as sailors might speak of a ship: the prison was a 'she' rather than stone, bricks and mortar. When I wrote to Atlé Dyregrov in Norway about this after the debriefing, he replied saying that in his work following other disasters he had found that the destruction of buildings was quite significant in causing traumatic reactions and he mentioned the destruction of houses, town centres and familiar buildings following earthquakes. We can become attached to people, but also to objects and things, so that they become an important part of ourselves and our lives.

In the second session, after a tea and coffee break, they spoke of the importance of emotional and physical contacts. One chaplain said that when he went home on the first day, he had a very strong sense of belonging to and of being loved by his own family. Another said that being given a hug at the time by another member of staff had given him great comfort and strength. They spoke about the incongruity presented by what it had been like in the prison before the riots broke out: what happened in the chapel and prison when the riots began; standing outside the prison for the next three weeks; being at home with their families at night with an overall feeling of confusion and disbelief intruding during the whole period of the event. The members of the chaplaincy team who had not been in the chapel when the riots broke out talked about feeling guilty that they had not been hostages with their colleagues. Whether hostages or not, there was a very strong sense of belonging to a caring, effective and supportive team and they said that being in the debriefing was helping them to hear and understand what it had been like for others. Some were slightly afraid when the riots broke out but did not believe or think that they were in danger of their lives, although they knew that physical violence against them was a possibility because it was happening all around them. After this session, the afternoon was free for them to go for a walk, talk together, read, remain silent or do whatever they wished.

The third session took place that evening and centred on various questions: what were you doing when the riots broke out; what were your thoughts at the time; what were your expectations and how prepared were you for what happened; what did happen and what were your experiences? Reactions were strong: there was a powerful feeling of unreality and some said that it felt like being in a game or circus in which staff and chaplains were pawns in a mad game, especially as some of those rioting were seen, not only as prisoners, but also as friends. One said that, after the riots broke out and they had left the chapel, a prison officer had told him in no uncertain manner and in language which he couldn't repeat, to pull himself together if he was to be of any use to them. He said that this was a salutary and good learning experience. The riots had continued for just over three weeks so reactions had changed over that time from initial disbelief and confusion to an increasing sense of anger, frustration and a gradual acceptance of what was happening, yet still not believing it! They were witnessing the destruction of their life's work, and, being mainly clergy, there was also the feeling and belief that they must have failed in some way.

On the second day the fourth session took place in the morning. What emerged as an important factor was that the riots took place over Holy Week and Easter. One chaplain said that he could not sing the words of any Easter hymn on Easter Day because he felt that in his mind it was still Good Friday, but he had nailed a palm cross to the prison gates! On a number of occasions, some had the feeling that they needed to be clean again and one went home on the first evening and changed the sheets on his bed. Sensory impressions were important and the sights they saw and the things they heard were indelibly printed in their minds. One major sense talked about was the smell, most of which came from the chapel being burnt down: the smell of burnt and damp wood. They also discussed what they were feeling now. Reactions were similar to those following bereavement with feelings of loss, frustration, helplessness, failure, guilt and blame, isolation, self-reproach, depression and sadness.

The fifth session was fairly general and allowed people just to say what they wanted to say, rather than being asked questions. There was some very cathartic, but mild swearing and some said that occasionally being told to 'Fuck off' by prison officers had caused much laughter and made things seem more real and human. They said that at the time this was helpful because it brought them from a phantom world into reality. All said that the Chaplaincy team had been drawn closer together by the event, and also by the debriefing, and was now much stronger and more supportive. One incident caused a pause for thought but also much laughter and amusement.

One chaplain said he had received dozens of letters of sympathy and support from Christians in churches, some from many miles away, one letter saying that he should remember what was said in the Bible in the letter to the Romans, chapter eight, that 'all things work together for good for those who love God'. He said that rather than comfort him this had made him extremely angry because he felt that, under the circumstances, it was meaningless and that the writer did not know what he was talking about and did not understand or know how he, the chaplain, was feeling. He added that he was also angry with himself because he had sometimes used the same quotation in his work with others! He laughed about it and said that it was a useful learning experience about sympathy and empathy.

One major effect of the incident, but also of the Debriefing, was that they felt that their team spirit was renewed and had given them a new confidence in themselves, in each other and in members of staff at the prison. They had discovered their own weaknesses but had received a new strength, especially through their sense, discovery and exploration of their own vulnerability. I then spoke of the normality of their reactions and feelings and that these two days were not the end. In the future they needed to monitor themselves and their colleagues and that there were channels for support if needed, with the rider that some of the support would come from their colleagues, team members and families as well as from other members of the prison staff. A final memory made us all smile: someone said that there was a notice pinned to the prison gates simply saying, 'Slightly Damaged Premises for Sale'.

I felt that I had used a new and exciting approach which had provided a safe, useful and appropriate model for helping them, both as individuals and as a team. All had responded to the model and were able to talk freely and openly. This was different from any approach I had used as a trained counsellor but it had felt exactly right. It is almost trite to say that 'it worked like magic', but that's how it felt. I had known exactly what procedure to follow and the model had provided an umbrella of safety under which we could all work together.

A major point about using Dyregrov's model, which I found useful, is that his model starts with an exploration of what was happening before the incident took place. This was important because when people have had a traumatic experience, most want to jump straight into the event and talk about what has happened. Dyregrov's model moves people from a place of safety, or relative safety, where they might or might not have been expecting anything to happen, before the incident, into and during the incident and, finally, into a place of safety afterwards.

This **before – during – after** model, used with cognitive reframing skills, described later, can enable people to see that their reactions result from the incident rather than from any weakness or fault in themselves. It is quite satisfying to see the light of knowledge, relief and comfort in the eyes of someone who is traumatised when they hear and realise this. It isn't the end of any problems but is an important insight in the journey towards recovery. Strangely enough, although the model requires the debriefer to very carefully direct the debriefing, I did not feel that I was an 'outsider' or visitor or even someone leading the group. I was accepted as a member of a team and the sessions almost seemed to run themselves. This experience of Atlé Dyregrov's model of psychological debriefing was to be the groundwork and basis for much of my future work with traumatised people.

• Armed robbery – 1990

In the town where I was based in the army, I met the local chief superintendent of police at a party and had seen in the media that there had been an attempted armed robbery in a shop during which the armed robber was shot and killed by the shopkeeper. When I said that I had trained as a counsellor and helped people after traumatic incidents, he asked if I would see the man who had done the shooting, which I did and, again, I used Dyregrov's model. A short while later, I was contacted again by the police and asked to help following a vicious armed robbery at a supermarket in which a family were involved and held hostage over-night. I used Dyregrov's model with the whole family but also had further counselling and support sessions and contact with them.

Debriefing is mentioned by the National Institute for Clinical Excellence (NICE) in the UK. Their recommendation is that debriefing should not be used as a single intervention but should be used with groups and involves pre-incident education and the creation of what I call 'a climate of acceptance of the normality of reactions'. There should also be awareness of the need for monitoring reactions and information given about the availability of resources, for referral, support and help afterwards. However, I have conducted many single incident debriefings as part of the counselling process, which can entail more than one session. The Dyregrov model and cognitive reframing techniques, especially using the **before – during – after** structure, can easily be adapted for use within counselling. In any case,

with a single incident psychological debriefing there has to
be a process of preparation and, where necessary, on-going
contact afterwards as appropriate. I will say more about this
and the controversy over debriefing in Chapter 7.

• The military hostages – 1990

On 2 August 1990, Saddam Hussein's armed forces invaded
Kuwait. Many foreign workers in Kuwait were arrested and
taken as hostages into Iraq where it was feared that, should
Iraq be attacked, they would be used as 'shields' at military
and other important sites. There were some 85 military
families, including wives and children, from the UK with
husbands working for the Kuwaiti government, who were
taken as hostages into Iraq where the women and children
were separated from the men. Some members of this military
team were on leave in the UK and they set up a help-line
in the Ministry of Defence in London for their friends and
colleagues and to keep in touch with relatives at home. I was
asked by the MoD to go to London regularly to support those
who were manning the help-lines. There were strong feelings
amongst members of the help-line of fear and anxiety for the
hostages and anger and guilt that they had not been with their
colleagues but were safely in the UK when the invasion took
place. All, including those on leave in the UK, had lost their
homes and all their personal, precious and some irreplaceable
belongings. One woman became very upset during her
break and said that it made her angry and feel awful when
she thought of soldiers, not only strangers but those who
were responsible for their plight, looking at photographs
of her teenage daughter and handling and stealing all their
private and personal possessions. Being a member of the
help-line was not an easy task for them and I became aware
that, if and when the hostages were released, there should
be some kind of gathering or reunion and opportunity for
them all, hostages and help-line personnel alike, to talk
together about what had happened. In late August, due to
the intervention of Ted Heath, the women and children were

allowed to return home and a meeting took place in the MoD between all interested parties to decide what should be done when they returned. My suggestion of a reunion and a form of defusing or debriefing was accepted and agreed and I was presented with the task of forming and training a team of debriefers. The debriefing team were selected and consisted of professionals who had counselling training and welfare experience: chaplains from the army and the RAF, a social worker and a Red Cross officer, both of whom worked in the army, plus two psychiatrists and a psychologist from the army medical services. Because of the timing and the availability of the debriefers, we had a day to prepare the team so we spent the time looking at Dyregrov's debriefing model using some role play and practice in groups and at the skills we would need in order to conduct the group sessions. We also had a session on possible reactions to a traumatic event. This was all a very hurried affair and, although we were a little nervous, we all felt confident that we could cope.

A day was organised for the hostages to meet at Bagshot Park, a lovely country house in Surrey belonging to the Queen and leased to the Royal Army Chaplains' Department at the end of the Second World War. This was a suitable place to hold the day: it was the Army Chaplains' home and a military establishment, which I thought was important, there was a relaxing and warm atmosphere in the house, the food would be good and there would be an opportunity to go for walks in the grounds and gardens. The day would also consist of experts being available to give advice on insurance, schooling for the children and housing problems. The main aim would be for the wives and older children to meet together, most having been split up both in Iraq and on their return to the UK, with some not knowing what had happened to the others, especially what was happening to their husbands who were still being held captive. There would also be an opportunity to gather in groups to talk about their experiences, fears and concerns using a simple form of debriefing based on the Dyregrov model.

However, there were some people in the armed forces who believed that any form of debriefing or counselling was a threat and who frowned upon anything psychological: it was unnecessary and would be a sign of acknowledging or even condoning weakness. The fear was that everybody might jump on the band-wagon! Early in the day, before the reunion started, I was approached by a senior army officer who said, 'don't you think you are trying to persuade these people that they owe themselves a problem?' I replied, 'do you mean that you think we are putting ideas into their minds?' 'Yes! he said. I then explained that we were not looking at what was not there but at what was there already! I then asked the officer who was introducing the day not to mention the word 'counselling' because debriefing was not counselling and mentioning the word might deter people from taking part.

He began by telling everyone gathered there that they were there to be counselled! Fortunately, in my introduction, which followed, I was able to say that the debriefing we were to use was not counselling and I explained the procedure, outlining what we would do in the group sessions. I added that the day was also organised to give them an opportunity to meet each other and to offer those who needed it advice about schooling, housing and insurance. I then said that we would put them into groups to discuss their experiences. There was an immediate response. Two women stood up and said that they would split themselves up into the required number of groups, which they did. I was pleased about this because it had shown that they had understood what the day was about and were willing to take part. The women, including some teenagers, organised themselves into groups and went into separate rooms, each with two members of the debriefing team to work through the simple debriefing process. There was a session before lunch and a session in the afternoon with time for them to meet together informally. As we had an odd number in our team, I decided not to take a group but to wait in the lounge in case anyone left their group, perhaps in distress. About three minutes after the beginning of the group sessions, one of the wives came storming into the central lounge from her group saying to me very angrily that this was ridiculous and under no circumstances did she wish to talk about what she had been through or was feeling or thinking. I got her a cup of tea and we sat down. I asked her what had happened and there was a stunned silence as she glared at me. She then began to talk and didn't stop talking for over an hour and a half about what she had been through! I nodded my head most of the time but was able to ask questions. She said that she had found it helpful to talk! When the day was over, I met with the debriefers and all agreed that they had found their group responsive and felt that it had been a useful and positive day. Over the next few days I received a number of telephone calls and letters from those attending saying how helpful it had been. However, we made one mistake: for lunch, we gave them chicken and rice and some said that this was what they were given frequently in Iraq!

We then learned that the men were to return home, which they did some weeks later, so I asked for a similar day for them, but this was not thought necessary. I did wonder if this was because they were men and therefore wouldn't suffer from stress! Eventually they did have a meeting where we were given a thirty minute slot with them, so I asked the psychiatrist and psychologist from the debriefing team to speak, with me, for ten minutes each. The psychiatrist mentioned that they might have difficulties in adjusting to being back with their families and, at one point, gently mentioned the possibility of sexual problems. Immediately, one man jumped to his feet and shouted out: 'We don't have any problems in that area, do we guys?' There was a pause – then a great shout from everyone present of 'Nooo!'

A few days later I was contacted by the MoD who said that they had decided that a debriefing day, similar to that organised for the women, would be organised. Over the next week I received a number of telephone calls from some of the men saying that they had wanted to come to the day but wouldn't attend. When I asked why, they all said that the letter they had received had stated that only those who were suffering need attend! I was not consulted about this day and not sent a copy of the letter. The day was duly cancelled! Is it surprising that nobody wanted to attend?

- The Army War Graves' Registration Team

When our involvement in the conflict in the Gulf was imminent, I was asked to spend a morning with the Army War Graves' Registration Team on their training course. This was a group of young men from the Royal Pioneer Corps who would have to deal with any dead bodies: our own, those of the enemy and, probably, of civilians. I began by talking to them about the importance and nature of the work and then split them into groups with a group leader and a 'scribe' to report back to the main group. I asked them to discuss and say what they were feeling and thinking about this task and to list what their concerns were. Every group produced a text-book list, especially of being away from their families and the possibility of having to deal with dead children or women or, perhaps, with someone they knew. Would they be able to cope or might they break down? How long would they have to do the work and how many dead people would they have to cope with? What about the stress and would they have any kind of support? They also listed possible emotional reactions such as shock, anxiety, exhaustion, sadness, depression and guilt and every group mentioned the word 'fear'. This caused a sudden explosion. An officer, who was in the room observing, jumped to his feet and, in a loud and angry voice, began to swear and berate them, saying that he didn't want to hear the word 'fear' and that they would just get on with the job and not complain – or words to that effect! I had, again, to stress the normality of any reactions, including fear, and the availability of channels for support, should it be needed.

On their return from the war, the debriefing team I had

trained conducted a simple debriefing with them. We split them up into small groups of five or six and used a shortened version of Dyregrov's model. The kinds of questions we asked them were:

- What were they thinking, feeling and expecting before they left home?
- What did they experience when they first arrived?
- What was it like within the first few days?
- What difficult experiences did they have and how did they cope?
- What support did they have from others?
- What were they thinking and feeling when they were ready to come home?
- What preparation did they have before returning?
- How was it when they returned home and how have they reacted since then?

There was a great feeling of support and comradeship, which was evident in the groups. In my group, at one point, a soldier, talking about some of the terrible sights he had seen and the difficult things he had had to do, broke down and began to cry. The reaction was quite moving. There was a quiet pause, but before I could say anything, a huge, 'hairy' soldier stood up, walked across the group, knelt down in front of him, put his arms around him and said, 'Don't worry, mate! You'll be all right!' There were similar instances in other groups of mutual empathy and support.

My main feeling was that these sessions had helped them to realise that they had done a very difficult and necessary job, that their reactions were normal and natural and that there were channels for help, should they need them. I heard much later, that when they arrived in the Gulf, the volume of their work was beyond what was expected so extra soldiers were drafted in from other units to help, apparently without having had any preparation or training. Our team did not meet with any of these 'extras' because, at the time, we did not know about them.

Shortly after the Graves' Registration Team training course involvement and before the war broke out, I went with the head of SSAFA social work and a senior member of the Red Cross, both civilians working in the army and who had been members of the debriefing team, to see a senior military psychiatrist and we suggested that in addition to their other training, soldiers might be given psychological educational preparation beforehand and, when they returned from the war, have some kind of defusing or debriefing and monitoring. We were also concerned about the effect on families. He was very polite, listened and took us out to lunch, but we never heard anything further. At this time, there was a feeling in the military at all levels, not by all of course, but quite powerful, that we did not need any psychological training or support. Some even denied the existence of PTSD. One army brigadier told me that, 'Unlike all Americans, we Brits do not have our own personal therapist!'

At a later stage, in 1991, before I retired from the army, I suggested to the MoD that one solution to the problem was to train specially selected personnel locally in districts, regiments and units who would be responsible for educating soldiers about the possible effects of stress, PTS and PTSD Using a form of assessment, such as simple defusing or debriefing, with groups and individuals, they could monitor soldiers during and after their return from deployment. They would be well-known and trusted members of their unit who would also be able to refer individuals and families to the resources for help and support where needed. Nothing came of the suggestion but this system is not unlike the Trauma Risk Management, or TRiM, procedure developed some years later in the military.

• Bomb disposal

I have worked with traumatised bomb disposal personnel but, because of the need for confidentiality, cannot give any personal details except to say that most were from experiences in Northern Ireland and the First Gulf War. It almost goes without saying that these were highly trained and very brave and courageous young men. However, as you would expect, some of the reactions experienced were similar to those of someone reacting to a traumatic event. At that time, one major factor is that, when defusing a bomb, as well as facing possible death, some bomb disposal personnel were totally encased in protective clothing, like a deep-sea diver of old. One officer said that he was particularly affected because he had never worn the full protective clothing until his first incident and that this had caused additional anxiety and fear.

Reactions were typical of traumatic stress: being afraid of making a mistake, anxiety, fear and feeling helpless, anger at the bomb makers, panic, isolation, flash-backs, dreams and sleeplessness. In the counselling sessions, some reported that, afterwards noises, such as cell-phones ringing, were particularly alarming and could result in a startle-response and that acrid and acid smells caused feelings of panic and brought back memories of the event in 'flash-backs'. Possibly because of isolation during the incident, some suffered from claustrophobia and anxiety when in enclosed or crowded places such as supermarkets. Others experienced agoraphobia, panic and fear when in open spaces. There were also reactions such as sweating, shaking, nervousness, pounding hearts and concerns about what would happen to their families if they were seriously injured or killed,.

In the next chapter, we look at the history of psychological trauma and the treatment of people who develop PTS or PTSD and describe these two conditions and their effects.

Chapter 4

TRAUMA AND THE MILITARY

Although this chapter concentrates on the military aspects of trauma, much of it applies equally to civilians who are suffering from stress and traumatic-stress reactions. They too can have the same reactions with identical problems for the individual, their families and all those involved with them

Stress, trauma and PTSD have been around as long as there have been people on earth because stress is a normal part of living. It enables us to stand up for what we believe and to protect ourselves and those we love but, if the stress goes beyond our ability to cope, it can lead to distress and eventual mental and physical breakdown. We all experience stresses of one kind or another, no matter how minor, and use certain strategies for coping. A 'Prayer for the Stressed' sums this up:

Lord, when I am having a bad day, Getting angry with people winding me up, Help me to remember that it takes twelve muscles to frown but only seven muscles to smile.

This appeared on the wall of an army sergeant's office, but he had added these words underneath: But only 4 muscles to stretch out my arm and smack someone in the mouth!

The number of muscles needed might be incorrect but the sentiment is familiar! However, there are still people who say, 'what happened to the good old British stiff upper lip?'

Is trauma a modern invention and disease? Definitely not! Many examples from ancient history to the present day show that traumatic stress is far from new.

• **William Shakespeare:** in Henry 4th Part 1, Act 2, Scene 11, Hotspur's wife is talking about him as he sleeps following combat:

> Why dost thou bend thine eyes upon the earth, and start so often when thou sitt'st alone? In thy faint slumbers I by thee have watch'd and heard thee murmur tales of iron wars and thus hath so bestirr'd thee in thy sleep, that beads of sweat have stood upon thy brow, and in thy face strange motions have appear'd, such as we see when men restrain their breath.

She then talks about the effect on their relationship. Hotspur avoids eye contact, has a startle-reaction when alone, murmuring in his sleep and possibly dreaming or having a nightmare, sweating and his face moving as though he is unable to breathe.

• **Samuel Pepys:**   in his diaries, mentions having traumatic reactions during and after the Great Fire of London in 1666.

• **Charles Dickens:** was involved in a train crash on 9 June, 1865, at Staplehurst in Kent, where 10 people died and 49 were injured. He was regarded as a hero because he had helped dying and injured passengers. Later, when recalling and writing about the incident he wrote,

> In writing these scanty words of recollection, I feel the shake and am obliged to stop ... I have sudden vague rushes of terror even when riding in a Hansom-cab, which are perfectly unreasonable but quite insurmountable.

Charles Dickens' daughter wrote: 'We have often seen him fall into a paroxysm of fear, tremble all over, clutch the arms of the railway carriage, large beads of perspiration standing out on his face.'

The movement of a Hansom cab mirrored the movement of the railway carriage and the feelings which were experienced in the crash were resurrected. His son said that this experience haunted him for the rest of his life.

These are early examples of what we would now call post-traumatic stress reactions, or even post-traumatic stress disorder, but we can go even further back in history.

• **Herodotus – Fifth Century BC:** The ancient Greek historian Herodotus tells the story of a battle in 480 BC, where a soldier called Aristodemus, who suffered from inflammation of his eyes, reported to the doctor. Because of his reactions he was called by his comrades 'Aristodemus the Trembler'. He never took part in the battle and, in shame, he went and hanged himself. Herodotus also writes of the battle of Marathon in 490 BC where a soldier called Epizelus was in the forefront of the battle and was proving to be a fierce and courageous warrior. He was suddenly struck blind, even though he had not been hit on the head or wounded, and he remained blind for the rest of his life. Epizelus said that he suddenly had a vision of a huge soldier with a long beard facing him, but who ignored him and killed the man standing next to him. It is possible that his loss of sight, had it occurred in the First World War, might have been diagnosed as 'hysterical blindness'.

❖ The Napoleonic Wars – Nineteenth Century

It is reported that the Duke of Wellington said: 'All soldiers run away. The good one's return!'

Sir Thomas Picton, a general who was killed at Waterloo, wrote to Wellington saying, 'My Lord, I must give up. I am grown so nervous that when there is any service to be done it works upon my mind, so that it is impossible for me to sleep at nights.'

Baron Dominique Larrey, Surgeon General to Napoleon in the Napoleonic war, treated psychological casualties, usually described as suffering from 'nostalgia', using exercise and music.

❖ The American Civil War – 1860s

Soldiers who suffered emotionally after battle were often diagnosed with 'soldiers' heart', sometimes called 'irritable heart' or 'Da Costa's syndrome'. Typical reactions were shortness of breath, headaches, sleep disturbances and impaired concentration. 'Nostalgia' was also used and even though reactions were seen as largely physical, some believed that these young men just wanted to be back home 'with the comfort of momma's apple pie'. At the end of the Civil War, the US Pensions' Board described one soldier, suffering from physical and psychological reactions by saying, 'After the war he was not worth anything. He was a lunatic!' In the 1880s, William Hammond, a doctor who had served in the Civil War, suggested that psychological casualties should be treated near to the front and this approach to treatment was mirrored and used in the First World War and later conflicts.

❖ The Second Boer War – 1902. 'Breaker Morant'

The Australian soldier, Lieutenant Harry 'Breaker' Morant, named for his skill with horses, served in the Bushveldt Carbineers in the Second Boer War. He was executed, with his friend, Lieutenant Peter Handcock, by firing squad on 27 February 1902 for the alleged killing of Boer prisoners of war and a Dutch clergyman. George Witton, one of the accused who was not executed, said later that Morant was so devastated by the death of Captain Hunt, his commanding officer, that he became like 'a man demented' and even broke down when addressing his troops. It is possible that he was suffering from traumatic stress because Morant believed that Captain Hunt, who was wounded and captured by Boers, was executed. Some believe that Morant and Handcock were shot as scapegoats, to appease growing concern in Europe about the atrocities committed during the war. George Witton later said:

War changes men's natures. The barbarities of war are seldom committed by abnormal men. The tragedy of war is that these horrors are committed by normal men in situations in which the ebb and flow of everyday life have departed and been replaced by a constant round of fear and anger and blood and death. Soldiers at war are not to be judged by civilian rules.

Although Harry Morant and Peter Handcock, as far as we know, were not suffering from PTSD, although Harry Morant might have had post-traumatic stress, George Witton briefly and admirably describes what war is like and how it can affect those involved.

❖ The First World War

Soldiers' heart, sometimes diagnosed as DAH, disordered action of the heart, was still used in the First World War as a diagnosis with the more familiar shell-shock, hysteria, neurasthenia and war neurosis, and words such as 'malingering', 'cowardice' and 'funking' were common. Some have claimed, perhaps cynically, that soldiers suffered from shell-shock while officers had neurasthenia and there might be an element of truth in this distinction. Some officers, like 10 per cent of aircrew in the Royal Flying Corps who suffered from stress and exhaustion, we might now call it Combat Stress, PTS or even PTSD, were usually sent home for rest or treatment when they could have been called cowards or accused of 'funking it'. One of my hobbies is First World War aviation and it concerned me when I read that some of these RFC officers sent home became flying instructors!

The word 'hysteria', frequently used to describe reactions, comes from the ancient Greek word 'husterikos', meaning 'womb'. It was once thought, because more women suffered from the condition than men, that the cause of hysteria was due to disturbances in the uterus. Was using the word 'hysteria' suggesting that a man was behaving like a woman? Over 3,000 men were sentenced to death in the war and approximately 10 per cent were executed. There seems little doubt that many who were executed in the First World War, the majority, over 260, for desertion and not cowardice as is often mistakenly thought, were suffering from reactions which would almost certainly now be diagnosed as combat stress, post-traumatic stress or post-traumatic stress disorder. As well as desertion, executions were also carried out for casting away arms, striking a superior officer, mutiny, disobedience, murder, sleeping at post and quitting post. Figures for those executed vary: for the UK, some give the figure of 306, although some reports say that 346 British and Imperial personnel were executed. Canada executed 25, New Zealand 5, the French around 700 and Germany 48. Australia refused to execute any soldiers. In 2006, after much lobbying, the British government gave a pardon to all British and Commonwealth personnel who were executed. The Defence Secretary, Des Browne, said;

I believe it is better to acknowledge that injustices were clearly done in some cases, even if we cannot say which, and to acknowledge that all these men were victims of war. I hope that pardoning these men will finally remove the stigma with which their families have lived for years.

From the beginning of the war in 1914 until April 1916, although the figures are controversial, it is estimated that approximately 1,300 officers and 11,300 other ranks were diagnosed with 'shell-shock'. During the entire war, some estimate that the numbers suffering from shell-shock was as high as 200,000.

• Treatment in the First World War

During the First World War much work was carried out by doctors and psychiatrists in treating psychological casualties and special hospitals were opened, such as Craig Lockhart Hospital near Edinburgh where Dr William Rivers, an army medical officer, worked with men who developed shell-shock, including the poets Siegfried Sassoon and Wilfred Owen. In spite of this, there was still an underlying belief in many that these people were malingerers, weak-minded or cowards.

Treatment was varied: the use of discipline, milk diet, hypnosis, sleep therapy and sedation for long periods of time, electric-shock sessions, rest and recuperation, exercise and, by some, like Dr William Rivers, the fairly new 'talking therapy'.

In February 1918, Dr Rivers, in the medical journal *The Lancet*, wrote:

The advice which has usually been given to my patients in other hospitals is that they should endeavour to banish all thoughts of war from their minds. In some cases, all conversation between patients or with visitors about the war is strictly forbidden, and the patients are instructed to lead their thoughts to other topics, to beautiful scenery and other pleasant aspects of experience.

Don't talk about it and think happy and peaceful thoughts! We have heard this advice before: 'Put it behind you and get on with your life.'

In 1923, Dr William Rivers suggested that officers might react to trauma in different ways from soldiers. He argued that private soldiers belonged to a social group in society where physical symptoms were more acceptable to them than psychological ones. He mentions occasions where soldiers lost the ability to speak and said that since soldiers were not allowed to say what they were thinking, they might react by becoming totally mute. Officers were more likely to stammer because, generally, they were allowed to express their opinions, but if they did, it would be breaking their code of behaviour and could be seen as criticising the system, leading to a lowering of morale. Dr Rivers believed that traumatic reactions were caused by the original battle trauma and, generally, not by any particular failure or weakness of the sufferer.

In 1916, Dr Charles Myers stressed the need to treat shell-shock and psychological casualties near the front line and set up special 'Advanced Sorting Centres' in the army rear area. Previously, some sufferers were sent back to hospitals in the UK, where it is said that many never recovered. Dr Myers used hypnosis and psychotherapy as treatments and believed that if patients were 'reunited with their memory', their physical symptoms would disappear. Because of these new centres, the return to duty rate amongst soldiers rose from 50 per cent to 90 per cent. However, Sir Arthur Sloggett (perhaps an appropriate name), the Director General of Army Medical Services, was against this development and, apparently, said, 'We can't be encumbered with lunatics in the army rear areas'.

Dr Thomas Salmon, in the US Army, said that much could be done in dealing with shell-shock cases if they could be treated within a few hours. He used four basic principles:

- **Immediacy**: be proactive and begin treatment as early as possible.
- **Proximity**: symptoms should be recognised and treated in the combat zone.
- **Simplicity**: make the casualty comfortable and give them rest and good food.
- **Expectation**: give reassurance and confidence in the treatment.

The French military had special centres close to the front lines for treating psychological casualties and it is claimed that 91 per cent of French soldiers who were treated this way returned to their units.

This early treatment, close to their units and near to the front line, was to be the basis of treating military personnel suffering psychological reactions, as will be shown later when describing treatment and the IPE (or PIE) system of Immediacy – Proximity – Expectation.

This system also had its roots in the 1880s in the work of Dr William Hammond, mentioned earlier. There was also concern about the character and approach of medical personnel. Dr William Johnson thought that the personality of the medical officer was of greater importance than any method used and research in recent times suggests that approximately 40 per cent of the success of any therapeutic intervention is due to the character and personality of the therapist rather than the method used. Following a traumatic experience in Northern Ireland a soldier who developed PTSD said that when he finally screwed up the courage to go to see a military psychiatrist and walked into the consulting room, it was the first time that anyone had treated him like a human being!

• Who or what is to blame?

There has always been an attempt to understand whether or not such psychological and physical reactions are caused by external events or are the fault of the sufferer, who was occasionally labelled as a coward, a degenerate or a mentally and physically weak individual. In 1896, a Dr Coulston said:

> If a man's brain is sound he can withstand any degrees of psychological stress. Only those whose brains are weakened by hereditary taint or the ravages of a debased life-style are tipped into insanity by external events.

So, is it the event or the individual? Concerns were, and still are today, often centred on the words 'cause' and 'compensation' – 'they are doing it for the money', with some blaming the individual and others blaming the event. In the First World War an army chaplain, Padre David Railton, wrote home saying:

> No words can tell you how I feel, nor can words tell you of the horrors of clearing a battle-field. This battalion was left to do that and several men went off with shell-shock.

I am certain that the shell-shock was caused, not just by the explosion of shells nearby, but by the sight, smell and horror of the battle-field in general. I felt awful.

In spite of this insight that it was the dreadful and horrific situation which was causing the problem, there was little use of the word 'fear', possibly because of a cultural belief that 'real men' should not be frightened or admit to being afraid. Before the first Gulf War, a brigadier in the army told me that soldiers should not be told that they might be frightened because, he said, 'If you do tell them, they will be afraid'. I replied, 'So if you don't tell them, they won't be frightened?' There was no reply as the brigadier walked away. The old soldiers' response to this remark is: 'Don't ever go to war with someone who isn't afraid – he'll get himself and you killed!'

❖ The Second World War

At the beginning of the Second World War, there were approximately 120,000 people receiving pensions for psychological problems from the First World War. Combat stress reaction and combat or battle stress were well known in the Second World War and later conflicts but, in spite of the fact that more than 118,000 men were discharged from the British army for psychological problems in the Second World War, words such as 'cowardice' and 'funking' were still used, again, in the belief that real men don't break down when under stress. This was typified by the use of the term 'LMF', 'lack of moral fibre', used in the Second World War by the RAF, especially for air crew from Bomber Command who developed psychological problems. Bomber crews were usually expected to fly thirty missions before they were given rest and if they broke down before then, most were immediately removed from their squadron and station in the belief that they might infect others, and were usually humiliated and reduced in rank. Immediately removing men who developed LMF from their comrades was supposed to deter others from developing it. An RAF sergeant who was diagnosed with LMF was seen by a psychiatrist and, after consultation with his aircrew who agreed to have him back, was given another chance. He went on to finish the missions, during which he won a medal for bravery when he rescued someone from a burning aircraft.

• John – the Dunkirk veteran

After I retired from the army in 1992 I met a GP who had been my civilian doctor. He asked me what I was doing and when I mentioned PTS and PTSD said he had heard of them and asked me to send him some information, which I did. A few days later he rang me and asked me to see a patient he was treating for depression, anxiety, sleeplessness and bouts of anger and said he thought that he might have PTSD. The man agreed to see me. Some of the information mentioned here was given by his wife.

John joined the army in 1933, was an ex-regimental sergeant major and a Dunkirk veteran. After he returned to England following the trauma of the evacuation, he had a 'nervous breakdown'. His symptoms were withdrawal into a protective shell, reporting sick frequently with seemingly minor illnesses and complaints, nightmares, bad dreams, and shaking fits. After his evacuation from Dunkirk, he was put into a 'mental asylum' where he was referred to as 'laddie' by medical staff. He said that the man in the next bed didn't just think he was Napoleon, he was Napoleon! On his first day he was taken to see a psychiatrist and walked into a large consulting room with a very high ceiling, where the psychiatrist was sitting behind a huge wooden desk. He was ordered to take off all his clothes and to stand at attention. John stripped to his underpants and stood there but the psychiatrist said angrily, 'Laddie! I told you to take off all your clothes'. Standing to attention, completely naked, he was then subjected to a series of questions beginning with: 'What is it that lives in a tree in the jungle and swings from branch to branch going 'uh-uh-uh-uh-oo' and eats bananas?' The next question was: 'What is it that has horns, eats grass and produces milk?'

A number of similar questions followed. John said he believed that this whole procedure – the size of the consulting room, the height of the ceiling, the huge desk, the stupid questions and standing naked – was done in order to humiliate him. When he recovered, he re-joined his unit after which he had occasional bouts of depression and illness but went back to serve in France and Germany after the D-Day landings. He said that after D-Day, one particular experience was the worst he could remember: a friend was killed next to him by an anti-tank rocket and had half his face blown off. He also remembered dragging burnt bodies through a wire fence but couldn't remember where he was at the time. After retiring from the army in 1962 he continued to work for the Ministry of Defence but he was still having occasional bouts of depression, anger, resentment and bitterness and suffering from sleeplessness and nightmares. His wife said that the periods between these attacks were becoming shorter and the symptoms stronger as he grew older.

After seeing him, I spoke to the GP and said that I was convinced that John was suffering from PTSD. He was referred to a psychiatrist, diagnosed with PTSD and received a bigger war pension. Sadly he was increasingly forgetful and eventually couldn't remember much and sometimes didn't know who I was so it was impossible to use any therapeutic approach except to visit him as a listener and friend, where he would sometimes get upset and talk about his war experiences. He told me that his nightmares consisted mainly of the same dream, in which he was lying on the floor in uniform in a huge room with a high ceiling with soldiers standing around him, shouting at him and ordering him to do things. He would then wake up sweating and screaming, 'I don't want to do it. I don't want to do it'.

The only connections John could make with these dreams were the huge consulting room in the asylum with a high ceiling and the feelings of guilt and anger at many of the things he had been ordered to do as a non-commissioned officer, especially having to commandeer houses for officers' and soldiers' accommodation. Frequently, he had to order the German occupants, mainly elderly people and women and children, to get out. He said he found it very distressing to have to put them out of their homes onto the streets even though he was told that this was necessary and said: 'This has bothered my conscience forever.'

Also, if he turned the TV on and there was anything about the war or conflict, he would become very angry, agitated and distressed. Fortunately, his wife had been a nurse and welfare officer during the war and was superb at looking after him and for many years had endured and learned to cope with his very difficult behaviour.

In the retreat from and evacuation of Dunkirk, it is estimated that 10 per cent of casualties were from psychological problems. However, a highly competent GP had been treating John for many years for depression, anxiety and bouts of anger, which helped to reduce symptoms, but the cause was John's involvement in the Second World War, resulting in his subsequent breakdown and the development of PTSD. Although he had fairly mild symptoms when he retired from the army, they dramatically increased after his retirement, but this is not unusual because symptoms of PTS or PTSD can lie dormant and develop months and even many years later.

In the Second World War, military psychiatrists were deployed but there was still suspicion in some people that they might be bad for morale.

A story is told about General Montgomery when a psychiatrist was posted to his command. The psychiatrist was asked to report immediately to the general but when he marched into Montgomery's office the great man ignored him and kept on writing. He then looked up at the psychiatrist, stared at him and told him to leave. When the psychiatrist asked why he had called him in, General Montgomery apparently replied: 'I just wanted to see what a psychiatrist looked like!'

An apocryphal story? Perhaps not!

- Combat stress reactions – CSR

Combat stress reactions were identified and acknowledged in the Second World War and were similar to civilian reactions to stress and trauma.

Psychological and emotional reactions: irritability, apathy, confusion, anxiety, depression, acute sadness, guilt, helplessness, fear, physical, emotional and psycho-logical withdrawal and paranoid behaviour.

Physical reactions: abdominal pains, difficulty breathing, sweating, nausea, vomiting, fast heart-beat, restlessness, startle reactions, a catatonic state, running away or wanting to run away, crying, manic behaviour, aggression and violence. The individual became a threat not only to himself, but also to others, and had to be removed from the combat zone.

It is reported that following the D-Day landings a psychiatrist in the US army would sit, usually in the evenings, with those who had just been in combat and they would talk informally about their experiences of the day. The psychiatrist said he was convinced that those who attended these early, informal debriefing meetings coped better with future combat than those who did not attend.

In his book *Band of Brothers*, which was made into a very successful television series, Stephen Ambrose tells the true story of 'Easy Company', a parachute and infantry regiment in the US army. This select and elite group of men landed in Normandy by parachute early on D-Day and continued in combat, with periods for rest, finishing their war at Berchtesgaden, Hitler's Eagle's Nest, on the German-Austrian border. Their commander on D-Day was Lieutenant, later Captain, then Major Richard Winters. Ambrose tells the story of Captain Winters' visit, following their experiences of combat, to some of his wounded soldiers in the first-aid station, one of whom was Private Albert Blithe. Winters asked

Blithe how he was and Blithe said that he was there because he was blind. Captain Winters very calmly reassured him, told him to relax and not to worry, that he had a ticket out of the war, that they would get him back to England and that he would be looked after and be all right. As Captain Winters began to move to the next casualty, Blithe started to get out of bed and Captain Winters told him to stay where he was and take it easy. Remarkably, Blithe said that he could now see and he was returned to his unit. Richard Winters' comment was that this man had blacked-out from fear and only needed someone to talk to him and give him reassurance. This was probably an example of a psychosomatic reaction, sometimes referred to as hysterical blindness, but also of an officer's care and concern for his men. In this case, a few kind words and a calm, warm, sympathetic and confident reassurance worked miracles!

This is very different from the attitude of General George Patton in Sicily on 3 August 1943, when an incident almost cost him his career. The general was visiting a hospital and came across a soldier in bed who was crying. Patton apparently asked him what was wrong and the soldier replied: 'It's my nerves I guess. I can't stand the shelling'. General Patton went into a rage, called the soldier a coward and ordered him back to the front. It is alleged that he struck the soldier on the back of the head with his hand or glove. On the orders of General Eisenhower, the Commander in Chief, Patton later apologised to the soldier and staff for his behaviour. Patton, apparently, didn't believe in combat stress or a caring approach! However, in mitigation, Patton was a human being with the responsibilities of a general and we don't know what stresses he was experiencing at the time.

❖ PTSD 1980 – 2013

In the USA in 1942, an incident in Boston, Massachusetts – the Cocoanut Grove Nightclub fire – resulted in the deaths of some 492 people, many of whom were military personnel. Dr Eric Lindemann, a psychiatrist who specialised in bereavement, and Dr Gerald Caplan, discovered symptoms which were not unlike those of people who suffered from other traumatic events. However, after the Vietnam War, where it is estimated that 15 per cent of all veterans developed PTSD, the US Congress saw no reason to provide facilities for the thousands who were suffering psychological problems – combat stress was not included in the psychiatric manuals. It was increasingly recognised that the reactions of suffering Vietnam veterans were similar to those of people who had experienced incidents such as rape, serious traffic accidents, muggings, armed robberies, natural disasters, air crashes, floods, tornadoes, hurricanes and a difficult childbirth. Eventually, in 1980, a new term, 'post-traumatic stress disorder', was included in the 'DSM', the Diagnostical and Statistical Manual of Mental Disorders of the American Psychiatric Association: the psychiatrists' Bible. This stipulated the conditions necessary for diagnosing PTSD.

In May 2013, the new DSM-5 changed the diagnostic criteria and the main emphasis was placed on behavioural symptoms: cognitive difficulties, depression and strong bodily and sensory reactions.

In the USA there was concern amongst the military about use of the word 'disorder' because they said that it might deter members of the armed services from seeking help. It was suggested that using the word 'injury' instead of disorder' might reduce any stigma. Others said that calling it post-traumatic stress injury would not change anything: it was the military environment and the negative and unhelpful attitudes which needed to change, not the name. The military'should be an organisation where reactions to traumatic stress and mental health care are acknowledged and accepted and where suffering military personnel are encouraged to seek help.

➤ Diagnostic Criteria for PTSD

The criteria here are simplified: for details search on the Internet for DSM-5 PTSD.

Four criteria are listed for a diagnosis of PTSD:

1. Personal experience of threatened death, serious injury or sexual violation.
2. Witnessing a traumatic event or learning of a traumatic event for a close family member or friend: where there is actual or threatened death – violent or accidental.
3. Repeated or extreme exposure to details of a traumatic event – but not through the media, pictures, TV or movies – unless it is work related.
4. Symptoms are not the result of other illnesses, medication, drugs or alcohol.

❖ DSM-5 – May 2013

➢ There are four main diagnostic groups

1. The intrusive symptoms: at least 1 required

Spontaneous re-experiencing and intrusive memories of the event causing vivid, disturbing 'flash-backs', dreams and nightmares, loss of consciousness, distress at exposure to reminders and dissociation: feelings of unreality, dreamlike and distorted. These can come suddenly 'out-of-the-blue' but sometimes will be triggered by the sight, sound, smell, taste or touch of something associated with the event. Children over 6 years can react with repetitive play, frightening dreams and re-enacting the event in play.

2. Avoidance behaviour: at least 1 required

This includes trauma related thoughts and feelings with external reminders of the event, such as people, places, situations and objects, triggering reactions.

3. Negative conditions and mood: at least 2 required

An inability to recall major aspects of the incident, persistent distorted negative beliefs, blaming self or others, estrangement and isolation from others, a diminished interest in activities, people or events and an inability to feel positive emotions especially with family, friends and social contacts.

4. Arousal: at least 2 required

Irritability and aggressive behaviour, reckless or self-destructive behaviour, difficulty falling or staying asleep, hyper-vigilance and an exaggerated startle-response, difficulty in concentrating, outbursts of anger or violence.

➢ Criterion F

For a diagnosis to be made symptoms from the four main diagnostic groups must have existed for more than a month and there should be functional impairment, feelings of depersonalisation, detachment from self with feelings of unreality and desensitisation and that 'Things are unreal!' Also, symptoms can be 'delayed' and occur later than six months, or appear many years after an incident. Other associated psychological, physical and social reactions are also common: fear, feeling of pointlessness, anxiety, depression, shame, survivor-guilt, palpitations, sweating, exhaustion, sensitivity in crowds and normal life and an increased use of alcohol and drugs.

After the Vietnam War, the effect on individuals and families was devastating, some claiming that more 'Veterans' committed suicide than were killed in the war. Figures for suicide vary from 9,000 to 100,000 but the lower figure is probably nearer the truth. Whatever the total, many veterans who committed suicide had developed PTSD. Some left their families and work and 'dropped out' of society and became hippies, vagrants, criminals, alcoholics or drug addicts.

In the UK, during and after the Falklands' War in 1982, the Ministry of Defence, largely denied the existence of post-traumatic stress disorder claiming that 'acknowledging psychological problems would damage fighting spirit and be bad for morale and recruitment.'

Also, psychological problems were seen as the responsibility, not of the MOD, but of the individual and civilian agencies such as the NHS or charities. But there were signs that all was not well. A Royal Navy psychiatrist who had served in the Falklands' War reported that some veterans had developed psychiatric problems, but he was largely ignored.

❖ Gulf War Syndrome

This was a term, originally coined by the media, which emerged after the First Gulf War and has been compared with chronic fatigue syndrome. Sufferers claimed, and still do, that their symptoms were the result of a cocktail of drugs and chemicals used in the war: depleted uranium shells; vaccines given against bacteriological, biological and chemical warfare, typhoid, cholera, polio, tetanus and anthrax; anti-nerve-agent tablets (NAPs); the use of 'pyridostigmine bromide', known as the 'anti-nerve gas pill'; organophosphate pesticide sprays; Iraqi nerve agents and even paint used on vehicles against chemical warfare attack.

Some claim that these caused illnesses such as motor-neurone disease, headaches, cancer, heart problems, fatigue, cognitive problems, loss of short-term memory, tingling and numbness in the limbs, muscle aches and pains, skin rashes, asthma and breathing problems, sleep disturbance, breakdown of the immune system and that the syndrome laid people open to infection and caused neurological and physical damage. Others said that there was no such syndrome!

❖ Differences between PTS & PTSD

• Post-traumatic stress

This can be defined as the natural and normal reaction of normal people to abnormal traumatic events. Symptoms can be experienced immediately, during or after a traumatic event or can gradually emerge slowly over a period of time They can lie dormant and emerge months or even years later and be anything from mild to distressing and be similar to, or even the same as, PTSD but with symptoms gradually decreasing over time, and people usually recover. However, this does not mean that the symptoms will disappear. Reactions can return in the future as memories, with psychological and physical reactions, but they will not necessarily develop into PTSD. Also, PTS. is not diagnosed until symptoms have been present for more than a month and, in this first month, if the symptoms persist, the term 'acute stress disorder' (ASD), has been used.

• Post-traumatic stress disorder

PTSD is not simply an extension of PTS; reactions are different in quantity and quality and with PTSD they do not go away. Reactions can intensify and persist or might lie dormant and emerge months or even years later and, when they do emerge, they can devastate the lives of individuals and families.

❖ Court case 2003

In a court case against the MoD by over 300 ex-service personnel, claiming to be suffering from PTSD or 'Gulf War Syndrome', the judge ruled that: the MoD had no duty to identify sufferers so as to be able to treat them. Incredibly, he said that the onus was on the individual 'to make known their suffering even when they were not trained to do so'.

He judged that 'crown and combat immunity' also applied to training, deployment, and peace-keeping operations and that:

> when two or more members of the Armed Forces of the Crown are engaged in the course of hostilities, one is under no duty to care to another ... a soldier does not owe a fellow soldier a duty of care in tort when either (one or the other or both) are engaged with an enemy in the course of combat.

He also dismissed the evidence of a chaplain, me, who had suggested, before the First Gulf War, that soldiers be given psychological preparation, education, some kind of assessment and aftercare when they returned. The judge said that a chaplain's evidence was meaningless because, he said 'chaplains did not carry a responsibility for the health of soldiers'.

Apparently, he didn't know that a chaplain's work could involve in caring, generally, for the welfare of all personnel in a regiment or unit. His judgement contradicted the central military belief that 'welfare is a function of command' and although the judge would not intend this, his judgement could be seen as an insult to the outstanding bravery and conduct of armed service personnel in combat zones, especially in the caring, comradeship and mutual and personal support they have for their comrades. It also goes against the whole military concept of the responsibility and comradeship that, as a 'band of brothers', members of the armed services have for one another, whether in combat or not. Needless to say, the claimants lost the case.

❖ Who or what is to blame – asking the question again?

After the Vietnam War there was still concern about blame. The question was,'Could it be something to do with upbringing, personality and character?'

In the USA, some 15 per cent of all Vietnam veterans, not just of those who were physically injured, developed PTSD, and research suggested that about 60 per cent of these had similar backgrounds with some of the following in common:

- Dysfunctional families;
- Frequent truancy from school;
- Poor academic achievement;
- Often in trouble with the police and involvement in petty crime;
- Sexual experience at an early stage in life;
- Drug abuse;
- Inability to relate successfully to peers or the opposite sex.

However, this did not account for the other 40 per cent who had different, or what we might describe as 'normal', backgrounds. Also, if they were able, by use of these criteria, to stop recruiting people who had problematic backgrounds, either there wouldn't be any army, or it would be a very small one!

Research by Forces Watch in the UK suggested that the youngest and less well educated troops from Iraq and Afghanistan were most at risk of developing PTSD and that some 24 per cent reported behaving violently after returning home. They also claim that these younger veterans suffered twice the rate of post-traumatic stress when compared with the rest of the services and that the suicide rate amongst those under the age of twenty was three times that of civilians. In spite of these difficulties, my experience is that most people who join the army, no matter what their background, upbringing, age or experiences, find themselves in a new family and generally thrive within a military community and culture. There can also be other influences on how we might react during and after traumatic events.

- Nature: what we are born with – it's in our genes.
- Nurture: the influence of our upbringing.
- Life experiences: what we have learned in life, including any expectations, preparation and training.
- Other influences; physical and mental health at the time or later; learned coping strategies; what we think or believe; the influence and nature of any support during and after the event; the presence of journalists and the media.

All of these can determine how we interpret an event, including suppression and denial of reactions and dissociating, the nature and extent in time of the incident and the support received before, during and after the event. Perhaps most important is the way that our brains deal with the information they receive through the various senses. This will be discussed later.

Outlining the diagnostic criteria for post-traumatic stress and post-traumatic stress disorder leads us to consider the problems of cumulative stress and the effects of PTS and PTSD on individuals and relationships. Also, how are professionals such as the members of the three emergency services influenced by their work and experiences and what strategies do they use for coping? Are reactions always negative and destructive or are there positive outcomes for some? These questions we will look at in the next chapter.

Chapter 5

TRAUMA – EFFECTS AND COPING

❖ Cumulative stress

Cumulative stress is stress that builds up over a long period of time, varying from a few days to months or even over many years. It is by no means limited to military personnel but can be found in those who work in the emergency and rescue services, doctors, nurses, social workers and those in similar professions. It can also develop in many other people and situations: teachers, clergy, airline staff and overseas aid workers, during and after emotional, physical or sexual abuse and bullying and in abusive and difficult ongoing relationships. Any sustained pressure in any life situation can result in reactions which can be defined as cumulative stress. It can also be experienced in cases that might, wrongly, be viewed as minor stresses: where someone lives with a difficult or abusive partner or parent or works as a carer where the stress, very slowly, builds up over time. Symptoms of cumulative stress can be the same as or similar to those of PTS or PTSD, with the same physical, psychological and emotional reactions of exhaustion, shock, denial, numbness, anger, sleeplessness, bad dreams, suppression of feelings and emotions, bitterness, guilt, helplessness and depression. However, cumulative stress reactions can be more deeply entrenched and intense than stresses from short-term incidents and sometimes the stress can be kept under control for a long period of time - until it explodes! Emergency services' personnel, members of the armed forces or someone belonging to a group or team, might cope well for many years as long as they have the support, security and protection that comes from being within an organisation: the comradeship, macho image and friendship of colleagues; the uniform; a sense of purpose; the excitement of attending traumatic incidents; the adrenalin rush and the feeling of doing an important job. Also, living in a supportive family or community can help people to survive and cope. But suppressed reactions can emerge when support systems disappear or when a major life-change takes place, especially if it is traumatic. If the stress continues there can be severe depression and a 'breakdown' both mentally and physically and some psychiatrists say that in the case of long-term involvement in a stressful or traumatic situation, given time, any person will 'break down'.

• Cumulative stress reactions

• Reactions can be suppressed, just below the surface, or repressed even deeper inside. Some will be unaware of how they are reacting and claim that they are 'alright' and that nothing is wrong, although others might see that this is far from being the case. Some become increasingly isolated and withdrawn and claim that nobody cares about them and their difficulties. They might work on their own and have little to do with any social gatherings and wish to sleep alone and avoid any kind of physical or emotional closeness.

• There can be increased reactions, at home or work, of anger and aggression to events and incidents which might normally be seen as minor or trivial. This can result in sudden and even violent outbursts of anger and frustration or crying, shouting and screaming. Some become irritable and will easily take offence or will be cynical, bitter, and critical of others or will blame themselves, colleagues, organisations or anyone, even those who try to help them. Senior personnel such as supervisors or managers experiencing cumulative stress can be over demanding and difficult to work with and make life extremely hard and even impossible for others, yet not believe or acknowledge that anything is wrong. Also, hidden emotions and feelings can be directed at other people: 'I'm not the one with the problem. You are!' This can sometimes result in a physical and emotional collapse.

• There can be signs of depression and the belief that work and life has little or no purpose or meaning, with feelings of pointlessness and that work, family and life is without reason or aim. Some might see little point in working and become so depressed that they resign, seek alternative employment or are off work for long periods with 'stress'. They might even contemplate or attempt suicide and some will succeed.

• An inability to cope with pressure and some might respond with the 'flight, fight or freeze' reaction: retreating and running away from the person or situation, physically or emotionally; reacting with aggression and anger and frustration; being frozen with shock and disbelief. There can be repressed and controlled pent-up energy which emerges in behaviour which is destructive and inappropriate. Someone might appear to be totally in control, calm and relaxed, or they become silent, anxious, nervous and on edge.

• Some are unable to focus on what others are telling them and might not hear or understand what they are being told. Even simple instructions or intentions can be misunderstood and other people can be seen as unhelpful, uncooperative and unkind. Some find it difficult to concentrate and make decisions and this can be dangerous or even fatal for those in positions of authority or leadership.

• Physical reactions are common, especially feeling extremely tired and listless. This can result in wanting to sleep, yet not being able to do so, an inability to rest or relax and even hyperactivity. There can also be reactions such as headaches, tightness in the chest, palpitations and fear of having a heart attack, stomach pains and sleep disturbances. As with PTS and PTSD, there can be 'out of the blue' reactions which come without any trigger or warning, an exaggerated startle response, hypervigilance – expecting something terrible to happen at any moment.

Any of these reactions can be difficult, not only for the individual concerned but also for those around them. Partners, families, friends and others might need help in understanding reactions and knowing how to react or cope.

❖ PTS & PTSD – effects on self & others

Living, working or being with someone who is experiencing post-traumatic stress reactions or PTSD can be extremely difficult and sometimes impossible. Their reactions can result in misunderstanding, lack of positive communication, anger, rage, guilt, frustration and apathy, leading to a breakdown in relationships. Also some of these reactions can be found not only in people who have PTS or PTSD but can also be mirrored in those who have to live or work with them.

• There can be changes in the way people see themselves, their partners, families and friends, their work or the world around them. They can feel misunderstood, rejected and isolated and think that there is no hope for them, no future and that nobody cares or can help. Some will talk incessantly about the event or their reactions and this can become irritating and boring for others whose response might be to not listen but to walk away or ignore the person! This can cause a retreat into silence or an eruption of anger and aggression and a feeling that nobody can understand. There can be constant preoccupation with the incident, making collages with newspaper clippings or photographs, writing a diary of the event and its aftermath and effects and keeping drawings or photographs.

A married soldier from the First Gulf War kept a number of photographs he had taken during the war. He had moved into the spare bedroom to sleep on his own and, because of their horrific nature, kept the photographs in a locked drawer beside his bed. He said he didn't know why he had to keep them and didn't know what to do with them. His wife often asked him what was in the locked drawer and why he looked so anxious when she asked him about it, but he couldn't tell her. He was afraid that she might find the photographs or see him looking at them and think that he was mad or depraved. He felt that he had to look at the photographs to remind him of what he had gone through and wanted to talk about what he had experienced, but couldn't because he said that he might break down and cry or make a fool of himself in front of his wife, who wouldn't understand.

• Some will withdraw and refuse to talk about what they have experienced and this can be because of a number of fears or anxieties as loosely expressed by this combatant after the Falklands' War:

If I talk to my wife or to someone I love or know, they might think I'm pathetic. Other people cannot understand and they might become distressed if I talk about it and I don't want to upset them. If I do talk about it, I might become upset. I don't want to re-experience it and descend into becoming an emotional wreck again and be seen as weak.

The result was that he withdrew into a cocoon of silence where he felt safe, He refused to talk about the war and the gap between him and his family continued to grow. In desperation, his wife made him go for help and then became involved in his therapy.

• Nightmares and dreams can be anything from mildly disturbing to horrific, waking up in a sweat and panic and shouting or screaming and suddenly twitching or 'jumping' in bed. This can be frightening and is another reason for someone to sleep alone. However, for some, isolation might be a relief from possible conflict, embarrassment, confrontation and feelings of shame or guilt.

• Exaggerated startle responses can occur where someone reacts in a manner out of all proportion to what has happened to them. Normally, coming up behind someone and just touching them on the shoulder can result in the other person being slightly surprised and saying, Gosh! You startled me! Someone with cumulative stress, PTS or PTSD, might jump up and either scream abuse or assault you or they might burst into tears and run away or react with a grim and angry silence.

A familiar story is of the soldier, who has experienced combat, walking down the street with his friends when a car backfires, or there is a loud bang. He immediately drops to the floor looking around, believing that someone is shooting at him and he becomes a shaking wreck.

A Kenyan who worked in the British High Commission and lived not far from the US Embassy in Nairobi had gone to the site after the bombing and was involved in helping. He said that every time there was a loud noise near or in their home, his wife would jump with fright, expecting something awful to happen. She was at home, had heard the original explosions, thought that her husband might have been injured or killed and became a 'bundle of nerves'.

• There can be a feeling that life is a waste of time resulting in an inability to make even simple decisions, a loss of concentration and lack of interest in partner, family, work, hobbies or social occasions. Some might not see any point in getting out of bed in the morning or going to work. A clergyman who developed PTSD often hid in the attic of the church to avoid contact with anyone.

A fire and rescue officer came home after involvement in a serious incident where there were fatalities and refused to get out of bed in the morning. He said: 'What's the point of getting out of bed when you have seen what I have seen and been through what I have experienced?'

The result was total listlessness and an inability to carry on with his normal life. After counselling, he left the fire service and found a less stressful job!

• The opposite response of panicking, over-activity and manic or pointless behaviour can also happen when life seems futile and without meaning.

• Feeling vulnerable is common, resulting in fear and anger, believing that the same event will happen again and not being able to see any future. Research in the USA showed that some children who had been traumatised could not imagine growing up, having a job, being married or having a family. Some can believe that they will not live long and might expect something terrible to happen at any moment.

Following a traffic accident, Elizabeth said that when she walked down the high street in town she would begin to perspire and experience a rising sense of doom, disaster and helplessness. She would be convinced that something awful was going to happen before she reached the next zebra-crossing: something would fall on her from above or a vehicle would mount the pavement and kill her. When nothing happened, she breathed a sigh of relief but then experienced a rising belief that something would happen when she reached the next lamp-post. As she walked down the street, this cycle was repeated over and over again.

• There can be outbursts of anger and violence, usually directed against objects such as furniture and ornaments, but, occasionally against a partner, family member, friend or even a stranger. This anger can be verbal, physical or both and can suddenly erupt, for no apparent reason, or be a reaction to something which, to others, seems trivial. A soldier who served in Northern Ireland during the 'troubles' developed PTSD but managed to keep control of himself at work. His behaviour at home was very different. Every Friday, for their evening meal, he liked to have fish and chips. He came home from work one Friday when the meal placed in front of him was sausage, egg and chips. He jumped up, screamed at his wife and began to smash up some of the furniture. Eventually things became so difficult that his wife made him go to see the medical officer where he was referred to a psychiatrist for help.

• Feeling 'I am useless and hopeless' is common. Some will change jobs regularly or see no point in working, lose interest in hobbies or sport, want to move home, be dissatisfied with their present life, partner, family or friends and even desperately look for a new partner and new relationships. These reactions can be extremely frustrating, painful and distressing for all involved, and reactions, such as feelings of lack of worth and hopelessness, can be transferred to a partner who might also feel useless and hopeless at not being able to cope or help. Some will avoid anything or anyone to do with the incident: any who try to help, anything which might bring back memories such as people, newspaper and TV reports, videos, photographs or anniversaries of the event. Some will sleep alone and not get involved in family matters and will avoid close physical contact with loved ones, including children. These reactions can be ongoing and distressing.

Sandy had been a prisoner of war in the Far East following the surrender at Singapore. He returned home at the end of the war, six stones in weight, arriving at Southampton, where he was given a five minute medical and a train ticket to return to Glasgow and his wife. They had two children but, fifty years later, his wife said that he had never shown any interest in the children and never played with them. He had never hugged her or shown her any affection and had suffered from nightmares, depression, flash-backs and bouts of anger. Eventually his wife encouraged him to go to Combat Stress, a charity offering help to ex-service personnel with psychological problems, where he was given treatment. Fifty years after his return, Sandy's comment was that when he returned from imprisonment he should have been given some kind of support or psychological counselling. 'We had nothing', he said.

There are people living on the streets of our cities and towns who have dropped out of society and, if they have any, have left their families and employment. Some estimate that two out of five of these are ex-service personnel who might be suffering from PTSD.

• There can be a lack of concern or understanding about the reactions and problems of others and a minor concern, worry or anxiety expressed by someone else can be seen as trivial and result in outbursts of anger: 'You complain about that? That's nothing when you've been through what I've been through and seen what I've seen!'

Those living with someone suffering can also become indifferent and might eventually back away saying that they have tried everything, have had enough and that nothing works. Both 'victim' and helper can have feelings of shame and fear about their behaviour, especially guilt or feelings of a lack of ability, or perceived ability, to cope. Both can feel that, 'I should be able to do something about it! I shouldn't feel like this or be like this: there must be something seriously wrong with me. I must be going mad.' Survivor guilt can happen not only when you have survived but also if someone you love or a friend or colleague has survived an incident when others have not.

Two married soldiers, whose families were close friends and from the same regiment, lived next to each other in married quarters. One was killed in the First Gulf War, and the wife of the soldier who survived felt guilty because her husband had come home while her friend's husband had not. Others said that she should be thankful that her husband was alive but she said that whenever she met her friend, it made her feel sad, guilty, very uncomfortable and embarrassed.

• There can be an increase in the use of tobacco and alcohol and other more serious drugs, legal or illegal. These are often used as a form of escape from reality and from the pain of physical and psychological reactions.

A married soldier who had been in the Falkland's War developed PTSD and regularly smoked marijuana. His rationale for this was that when he used the drug, 'It's the only time I feel good!' The drug was used to take away the bad feelings but the result was addiction and the associated personal, physical, psychological and social problems. He eventually went to live on his own and became scruffy, unshaven and slouched when he walked. He was without hope and believed that nobody could understand or help him. He turned to drink and lost his driving licence because of being over the limit and his life gradually deteriorated. He found a job but couldn't cope and killed himself.

❖ General comments

Although some people might have only a few of these reactions, sometimes they will appear intermittently. As with bereavement, reactions can change from day to day and sometimes it doesn't seem so bad. One day there might be hope and the feeling that all will be well but the next day can be full of depression and despair and the following day of anxiety, helplessness and insomnia. It is important to stress again that those who live or work with someone who is suffering from stress, PTS or PTSD, can also feel and reflect some of the same reactions. It is normal to be angry, depressed and frustrated when living with someone who is angry or indifferent and unloving or who lives in a cocoon of silence and withdrawal.

Sensory experiences are especially important because they can trigger reactions with subsequent feelings of fear, panic, horror and disorientation. A sight, sound, touch, taste or smell associated with an incident can resurrect reactions resulting in flash-backs, re-experiencing the incident.

Ken was trapped in a car after a traffic accident, alone in the countryside, but not injured. The emergency services arrived, rescued him and took him to hospital for a check-up but he appeared to be all right. Next day, he borrowed his wife's car and went to fill it up with petrol. He put the nozzle into the tank, pulled the trigger and the smell of petrol caused him to panic and run around screaming. He said later that when he was sitting in the car, waiting to be rescued, he could smell petrol and hear the hot engine ticking away as it cooled. He thought that at any minute the petrol would ignite and he would be burnt to death. The smell of petrol had made him feel that he was back in the car and about to die.

This kind of experience can also cause avoidance behaviour where people from accidents or disasters might refuse to travel by car, train or air. After the Paddington train-crash on 5 October 1999, when 31 people died and over 520 were injured, some commuters to London from places such as Gloucester, Stroud and Swindon said that they were never going to travel on a train again and would look for a job locally. I don't know if anyone did this but it is a natural reaction to not want to do something which might cause further distress or injury.

Also, where a partner or friend has died there can be avoidance behaviour where someone develops an inability or reluctance to form or sustain relationships because of the fear and pain of losing someone again. Avoiding something which is distressing might be seen by some as a form of weakness or denial of reality, but it is a common reaction for people who have experienced a traumatic event. It needs to be stressed again that partners, families, friends and colleagues can also experience avoidance behaviour and develop reactions similar to those of the person suffering from stress, PTS or PTSD.

• Things sufferers can say:
'I just keep everything to myself and bottle it up inside. There's nothing I can do about it. It's not my fault, but I feel so guilty and can't control my emotions. I know it's distressing for my partner and family but I can't help it. Nobody can help me.'

'What's the point of trying? I feel so helpless now that this thing has taken over my life. I can't tell her what I went through. She wouldn't understand.'

• Things partners can say:
'He's a nightmare to live with. I get so depressed, angry and frustrated. Why should we have to put up with his behaviour? He's not the man I married!'

'It's the drinking, dark moods and the anger I can't stand. Sex has gone out of the window and he sleeps in the spare room. I don't want him near me.'

'He just lives in a world of his own. It's as though he's surrounded by a wall of silence. He ignores me and the children and I'm frightened of his bouts of anger and violence.'

However, there are many partners who do manage to look after the one they love, but it can be a struggle which some people just can't cope with or endure and, sadly, the breakdown of relationships is not unusual.

❖ Professionals – possible reactions

Members of the police, fire and rescue and ambulance services and other professional helpers are not immune to suffering from traumatic stress and although the tendency is for them to have a tough, male and macho image, it is generally recognised that they too can develop symptoms of stress, cumulative stress, PTS or PTSD. Most professionals cope very well and if any of the following reactions do occur they are usually temporary.

• Helplessness: rescuers and helpers expect to be in control of their physical and emotional reactions and aim to succeed in what they do. However, there will be times, even when they have done their best, that they can feel helpless and useless. There will be occasions when they are unable to save lives and might arrive at a scene where people are already seriously injured or dead.

• Fear and anxiety: there can be fear and anxiety that they might break down and not be able to do their job. This can be true of those new to the work but also of those who have wide experience and expect to cope. They might identify what they are doing or seeing with their personal lives and compare victims with other members of their own family, especially where there is a physical likeness: a similar age or physique or with the same colour hair or other similarity to someone they remember r from a previous incident. There can also be the thought: 'This could be me!'

• Unfairness and injustice: casualties can be seen as innocent victims of the insecurity of life and it can seem so unfair that people, especially children, should be injured or die. Events can result in professionals asking questions about the meaning and purpose of life: 'It's bad enough when anyone dies, but not children. Why do these things happen? It's not fair!'

In one incident, following a bus crash, members of the emergency services expected to find adults in the vehicle and probably would have been prepared for this. Arriving at the scene, they found that most of the passengers were children, some of whom were severely injured and others had died. Their expectations were shattered: officers were shocked and, because of their wrong expectations, they had to immediately control and adapt their feelings and emotions to their reactions.

• Anger: it is normal to be angry when something tragic happens and this can escalate into someone becoming irritable and intolerant both with themselves and with others. This can also be taken into home and family life with outbursts of anger and frustration, even when there is nothing to be angry about.

• Sorrow and grief: dealing with the aftermath of an accident or disaster can trigger feelings of acute sorrow and grief even when the victims are strangers. It can be difficult not to be upset or emotional, even for professionals, when there are fatalities and it is not unusual for some symptoms of bereavement and loss, such as sorrow and grief, to emerge.

• Intrusive thoughts and images: what we see, hear, smell, taste or touch in the past can trigger a response and influence how we feel and react now.

A Fire and Rescue officer was attending a road traffic accident where the occupants of a vehicle were burned to death. The smell was terrible. He said that after this event, even many years later, he could not eat roast pork because the smell brought back disturbing memories of the incident.

Thoughts and images from an incident, past or present, can intrude and have a disturbing or shattering effect leading to the asking questions of such as: 'Why am I reacting like this? Have I done enough, Have I failed?'

Professionals usually cope with these experiences and reactions but some such feelings and thoughts can still be present.

• Self-reproach, shame and guilt: as with previous reactions, these can emerge either at the time or later but, like other reactions, should be seen as normal and natural. Even when you have done your best, it is not unusual to think that you could have done better and done much more to help and to have feelings of shame and guilt. This can also include 'survivor guilt' which can be the result of the death of a colleague but can also come from seeing other people, even strangers, injured, dying or dead. There can also be similar reactions from non-professionals present such as reporters, photographers, spectators or civilian helpers.

After the Zeebrugge disaster on 6 March 1987, in which 193 people died, a member of the crew who survived went to the harbour and stood every day staring out to sea burdened by guilt that he had not done more to save lives. Another survivor, who had lost a number of family members, including his wife, desperately trying to make sense of the disaster, said that he was convinced that he had survived because he was the only one who could cope with what had happened! Physically and emotionally he looked absolutely terrible, utterly shocked, devastated and stricken with grief.

❖ Coping strategies of professionals

Civilians, military personnel and professional helpers, will use certain strategies in order to cope during and following a traumatic incident but how successfully they cope is the question. The following strategies can include the defence of 'dissociating', where someone is there physically doing their job but copes by distancing themselves emotionally from the incident. Some claim that there is evidence that 'dissociating' increases the possibility of the development of PTSD.

From research conducted by Dr Atlé Dyregrov in Norway, the following are strategies used by professional rescuers and helpers during and after traumatic events. They also include some of the strategies used by social workers, as I found in the month I spent with them looking at the problem of stress, in May 1992, just before I left the army. These are not necessarily separate coping strategies but are interrelated and individuals can and will usually use more than one strategy at any time.

• Being active: some will concentrate on the task in hand and ignore or be unaware of what is happening around them and can say 'I just got on with the job I was trained to do'. When there are problems, difficulties or traumatic events, some will say that action is the best way to cope. The point is, 'keep busy'.

• Giving mutual support: there is usually much talking, touching and physical contact between individuals, teams or groups, although some can isolate themselves from others and might become angry if others try to talk to them. However, the strong sense of belonging to an elite group and the camaraderie, plus their training, can bond people together into a team where it is natural and normal for mutual support to take place. They don't have to think about it because, 'this is what we do!'

• Suppressing emotions: some will make a conscious effort to control and suppress any emotional reactions or feelings and this is a natural coping and survival mechanism. It would not help if a rescuer ran away crying or screaming, so there is a need to control reactions and to get on with the job of rescuing and saving lives. Sometimes it is necessary to have a 'stiff upper lip' and a sense of duty and responsibility and these can help people to cope. But suppressing emotions can result in problems and the need for someone to talk to about their experiences.

• A sense of unreality: this is not necessarily a conscious reaction: it can just happen. Some will feel detached and say, 'I felt like an actor in a play', or, 'This is not real!' Others say that they sometimes have an 'out-of-body' experience, as if they are watching themselves from above.

• Avoidance behaviour: some will think of the bodies and victims as dolls or dummies and try not to think of them as real people. Some distract themselves by thinking of other things: the garden at home, what they are having for their next meal, a hobby or other interest or activity. Others might talk to themselves, sing or hum or repeat familiar poems or sentences, silently or out loud.

• Preparation: when hearing the news of an incident, professionals can begin mental preparation on their way to the scene by thinking of other and similar incidents in which they have been involved. They can ask, 'How will I react and will I cope now?' Again, a sense of professionalism helps. The Army War Graves' Registration Team for the First Gulf War said that their preparation and training had helped them to cope because it had given them confidence in themselves and in their colleagues. Training is helpful but occasionally the real thing comes as a shock, even to those with long experience. Also, expectations can be wrong and cause confusion and uncertainty, as mentioned earlier, where it was believed that the passengers in the bus crash would be adults, not children.

• Professionalism and training: training helps people to cope and usually gives them confidence in themselves and in their colleagues and engenders the feeling that 'I am a professional. I am trained to cope'. Knowing what to do, having personal and group confidence and colleagues around can help people to cope and survive. Wearing a uniform and working as a team with familiar apparatus and equipment can also create group solidarity and confidence and increase the ability to cope.

• Regulating exposure: leaders of professionals usually limit the amount of time workers are involved in an incident and ensure that they have periods of rest and refreshments, but not too long, or they might find it difficult to return. Alternatively, not returning, or returning to find that others have taken over the work, can cause frustration and anger. Military personnel returning from deployment in Afghanistan spend a few days in Cyprus, called decompression, where they can relax, talk, exercise and unwind before returning home. This can help them to get back into their normal lives.

• Having a sense of purpose: there can be the feeling that 'I have to do it, am trained to do it, and I will cope'; and in rescuing and saving lives there is a definite aim and purpose. But this can be influenced and affected by incidents where there is loss of life or where events have been caused by negligence or design. With the Army War Graves' Registration Team, everyone felt that one reason for doing the job was not just because they had been told and trained to do it, but because they would be doing it for dead colleagues and their families. During the debriefing when they returned, they said that his gave them a sense of purpose and helped them to cope.

• Humour: humour is a positive way of coping with trauma and is used by many emergency services' personnel, but most people use it as a method of coping. Many of the jokes we hear or tell and make us laugh are about scary things: the absurd, marriage, sex, death, anger, religion, war or other difficult aspects of life. Joking about these can enable us to cope with situations which might overwhelm us, especially if we were to think of families, relatives and friends of the victims. However, humour is not usually used when outsiders are present or following the deaths of children. Humour, even sick humour, is a method of pushing away and controlling painful feelings and reactions, but it can also be an attempt to escape from or deny them. When feelings and emotions are repressed, they might emerge as more serious problems at a later stage and, where humour is used most of the time, it can result in people becoming cold, cynical, insensitive and unsympathetic.

• Talking: some find that they need to talk, either during or after an incident and will share their reactions with others but some will react by not talking at all. This silence can be reflective but can also be a sign of shock or retreating into isolation and avoidance. Fire and rescue officers have a useful method of coping after incidents: they all go back to the station 'mess' where they have tea or coffee and something to eat and sit around and talk about what has happened. Talking to family members or colleagues, sometimes in the local pub with a friend, can be a useful form of very simple one-to-one or group defusing or debriefing.

After the Falklands' War it is said that those who travelled home by sea coped better emotionally, physically and psychologically than those who came back by air. On the ship, which took some days to sail home, there were many opportunities to relax and also to sit with their mates and talk, often over a few drinks in the bar. There was also the availability of the chaplain, doctor, psychiatrist or psychiatric nurse, all of whom would provide support, reassurance and a listening ear. They were also given information about possible reactions and avenues for help and to talk about getting back into their families. Those who travelled by air were home in a few hours and had little or no opportunity to do any of these things except talk to the person or persons sitting next to them. The lack of ability to relax and talk about their experiences could have made it more difficult for them to relate to their normal lives on their return home.

❖ Other strategies

After a traumatic incident some will listen to music, take exercise, use a hobby, drink alcohol or have some other means of relaxing and relieving the stress. When I was listening to social workers talking about coping with stress, one said that she lived alone and when she went home her way of relieving the stress and tension was to talk to her cat! Others said that they would talk to themselves or they would sing and shout loudly in the car on their way home, often wondering what other drivers alongside them at traffic lights were thinking! A few said that sometimes they were drinking more alcohol or smoking more cigarettes than usual and some said that they did not talk to their colleagues about their problems or stresses because they didn't want to worry them: 'My colleagues have enough anxieties and stresses of their own without also having to carry mine.' This could have reduced stress levels for others but, by not talking, might increase their own stress and they and others might believe that they are the only ones experiencing problems. It can be supportive to know that you are not alone in the way you are reacting and that others have similar feelings. This is one of the benefits of simple group defusing and debriefing techniques.

• Being grateful; some say that remembering how lucky they are helps them to cope, although this can result in feelings of guilt and even survivor-guilt. However, being grateful for surviving or being successful in their work can be very positive: it can be as simple as feeling it's good to be alive!

• Expressing emotions and feelings: some will need to express how they are reacting after an incident and this can be helpful, especially where it is understood by all that such reactions are not signs of weakness or inadequacy. However, there can still be the odd cynics who have little sympathy for the reactions of others.

A senior prison officer, known as a 'hard man', was involved in a violent prison riot and coped: his 'macho' image prevailed and he was superb in his role and responsibility. Everyone praised him after the riots were over. A few days later he was shopping in a supermarket, when he was suddenly overcome by the crowds and noise. He began to panic and fainted. He awoke, not knowing where he was, to find a little old lady, with a shopping basket, bending over him asking him if he was all right! Later, when he talked about this he realised that his response was triggered by the resurrection of his emotions and feelings created and suppressed during the riots: the noise and the crowds in the supermarket overwhelmed him.

But expressing emotional and physical reactions can be devastating. In the TV film Warriors, about soldiers in Bosnia serving with the United Nations forces in 1992, there is a scene where a soldier who is severely traumatised and suffering from PTSD is at home in Liverpool shopping in a supermarket with his grandmother. He stands and watches as a little girl has a tantrum in front of her mother, screaming and demanding sweets from the shelves. He suddenly bursts out in anger shouting that he has seen burnt and dead children and people. The little girl's mother is shocked and shouts at him saying that he is mad. He has to leave the store and his grandmother takes him home. On another occasion, while in a rage, he totally destroys a bus shelter.

Catharsis, expressing emotions and feelings, can help but there can be a right time and place to do it, but what does it matter if you are angry or burst into tears or collapse in a supermarket? It can be embarrassing and upsetting, but is not abnormal. But it is a much better strategy to realise that expressing reactions and talking about them can help, not only to enable feelings to emerge, but also to help to integrate the experience and reactions into one's life and personal experience. But as well as negative and unhelpful, reactions can also be positive.

❖ Positive reactions to trauma

Feelings and reactions after an incident can depend on a number of factors: the nature and extent in time of the incident, the training, character and experience of the individual, how they are treated at the time by colleagues and others, what support they might have had during and after the event and the positive or negative influence and involvement of the media. However, it needs to be stressed that most professionals cope most of the time and experience positive and helpful reactions and feel the satisfaction of a job well done.

There can be three major and positive reactions, as outlined by Dr Atlé Dyregrov in his research:

• An increased sense of value: there can be a very strong sense of having achieved something, of personal success and of having coped. Life feels more precious and valuable and the world is seen as a good place in which to live.

• An increased appreciation of personal life: some will say that they appreciate and value their loved-ones and family more than ever. 'When you see terrible things, it makes you realise how lucky you are and how much your family and friends mean to you. Life, love and friendship are the most important things in the world.'

• An increased sense of achievement: some will discover a new inner strength and sense of purpose and see others as more reliable and trustworthy and be surprised at their own ability to do the job and to cope. There can also be a deep sense of satisfaction and fulfilment and even feelings of euphoria, elation and excitement. However, these positive reactions might not be immediate but can come at a much later stage. In his research, Dr Atlé Dyregrov found that if positive feelings do come, it might be up to a year or so later. It is also worth remembering that some will not have any positive or negative feelings but might simply say: 'I was just doing my job and getting on with it'.

Why do people develop negative or positive reactions? Why can't we just accept what life brings to us and cope? The answer must be, 'because we are human!' But, there are clues as to why and how we might react, and this is discussed in the next chapter.

Chapter 6

THEORIES AND MODELS

Why do people react to traumatic experiences?

In trying to understand why and how you, or others, might react and how you might be helped, there are a number of theories and models which can throw light on the subject. They are all different yet have a similar theme, trying not only to understand reactions but also to understand where their basis might lie in the human psyche and experience. These theories and models might be helpful in self-understanding and also give clues as to why we and others behave as we do when under stress: they can help us to understand other people but also to understand ourselves. Some of them might not sound familiar but hopefully some of them will. They are theories and models and they apply not only to professional helpers and military personnel but to anyone who has a traumatic experience.

❖ Learned coping strategies

We might try to cope by using strategies we have learned from the past and these might help but, if the strategies don't work symptoms can increase, leading to confusion and fear, especially if we are using a strategy of which we are unaware. A better knowledge of these strategies can help us understand why we react in a particular way and sometimes enable us to adjust or change our reactions to a different and more positive way of coping. Robert is a typical example.

The Story of Robert

Robert was a pleasant, smart and quiet man, aged 34 years, working in a very ordinary and undemanding job. He was involved as a passenger in an accident when his father's car skidded off the road while attempting to take a corner at high speed. His father was uninjured but Robert broke his right arm and an ankle. This caused him pain and ongoing problems: he was unable to work for some time and the pain was a constant reminder of the incident. He was having bouts of acute anger and frustration and bad dreams and nightmares and couldn't understand why. He talked generally for a while about his present life, his work, hobbies and interests and discovered that he didn't have any hobbies or interests and he didn't have many friends! Using a simple 'before, during and after' process, he talked through the incident: before it happened, while in hospital and then up to the present. However, he didn't seem to be telling the whole story so I asked him how he was feeling. He said, quite calmly, that he was extremely angry with his father, who had been driving, but didn't know why. He also wondered if he was to blame in any way and if he was going mad. As he talked, he began to accept that he was not to blame, that feeling angry was common after such incidents, that he was not going mad and that, under the circumstances, his anger with his father was understandable. However, from his body language and the way he was speaking, I thought that his anger and dreams might not really be about the accident but about his relationship with his father. When asked about this, he stared at me, stammered slightly, took a deep breath, seemed to 'pull himself together' and said that he hated his father and had done so for most of his life. I asked him what he meant by 'most of his life'. He found it very difficult to reply but began to talk about his childhood and being sent away to board at prep school at the age of six. I asked how he felt about this and he said that he felt that he had been deserted and rejected by his parents, especially by his father who, whenever he was home from school either at weekends or during holidays, would be away and never spent any time with him. However, when his father was present, as far back as Robert could remember, he was extremely critical, demanding, bullying and verbally abusive. I asked him how he had dealt with this and he said, very calmly, that he had learned to control his emotions. During his first months at prep school he would lie awake at night in the dormitory, listening to some of the other boys sobbing and crying and he remembered putting his hands over his ears and saying over and over again, 'I'm not going to cry, I'm not going to cry!' This was repeated until he fell asleep. He also explained that when he went on to board at public school he used the same strategy for coping with any problems he faced: he buried his emotions and suppressed them. I asked him how he coped with difficult situations now. There was a long silence, he became quite emotional and said that he had begun to realise that he used this same strategy in his adult life: whenever he was aware that any feelings or emotions were rising, he would consciously and deliberately control his reactions and bury them away inside. However, he said he was beginning to understand that how he behaved now as an adult was the result of his childhood and upbringing and added that this learning was rather like a light being switched on in his mind. I saw Robert four times for counselling after which he felt that he could cope on his own, the bad dreams had disappeared and he was gradually learning to express his feelings. He telephoned me a few months later to say that he now felt very positive about his life, had a girlfriend and was moving on. He kept in touch for over a year.

From birth, we all develop learned coping strategies and sometimes these are not appropriate for the situations we face, yet we might continue to use them, sometimes with negative or even disastrous consequences.

❖ Object Relations Theory

About twenty-five years ago I came across a cartoon entitled 'Suddenly … You're a man!', but I can't remember where it came from. It shows a man ready for bed, obviously an adult male: he has a stubbly beard and hairs on his arms, ankles and stomach. He looks anxious: his eyes are small and close together; he is sucking his thumb and carrying a small teddy-bear; he is wearing pyjamas which are too small and have either shrunk in the wash or come from his childhood and his slippers have clowns' faces on them. I looked at it and, after smiling, realised that it was a cartoon which expressed something deeply significant about human nature. It was an image of many people I had counselled, but I also realised that it was an image of me! I don't suck my thumb, wear pyjamas that are too small, have a teddy bear or wear slippers with faces on them, but it shows something about human nature and behaviour. Here is an adult using strategies from the past to help him to cope with his present anxiety. Sucking his thumb takes him back to the comfort of his mother's breast and the pyjamas help him to feel safe like being a child again, protected and sheltered from the world around him. Psychologists call the teddy bear a 'transitional object', a term used by Dr Donald Winnicott, an eminent paediatrician and child psychologist who worked at Paddington Green Children's Hospital in London. This transitional object gives us a direct, concrete, physical and emotional link with the past, to a time when we were safe, and is representative of the closeness, comfort and intimacy we felt in early life.

From the 1930s until his death in 1971, Dr Donald Winnicott was also a specialist in the field of Object Relations Theory. Simply put, this is the theory that some things, such as toys, teddy bears, comfy-cloths and thumbs, even people and other objects, are not just physical things but can represent past and present experiences and relationships, especially the link with a mother or primary carer, and early upbringing. I am always moved and smile when I see a child in a supermarket or in the street, walking slowly along with thumb in mouth and towing or clutching a cloth or fluffy soft toy or a piece of material, usually part of a blanket or clothing.

This is a powerful symbol of a child relating to the past as well as the present and helping him or her to cope now and to move on into the future. A young mother told me that she was gradually cutting pieces off her child's comfy-cloth and was concerned as to how her child would react when it became the size of a postage stamp and then disappeared!

At home we still have a cloth toy called 'Panda' who is over 46 years old, bought for our first son. He is ragged and has been mended so many times that there is not much left of the original 'poor old Panda'. But he is still treasured and my two sons, as adults, when they came home, would pick him up, and, with a smile, smell him. Sadly, over the years he has been washed and cleaned so many times that the smell has disappeared!

At a personal level I discovered that I also use strategies from the past in order to cope with people or events. Because of incidents, from my childhood and teenage years, I had developed the strategy of sometimes calmly walking away and backing off when facing what I felt were threatening situations. I preferred the 'flight' rather than the 'fight' or 'freeze' reaction. It was only later in life when I trained as a counsellor that I recognised this and I found that acknowledging, knowing and realising it meant that I am more able to cope with such situations as I grow older. The point is that how we might react to a traumatic event can be determined partly by our childhood, upbringing and life experiences, but also that from our early life onwards, and throughout our lives, we learn certain coping strategies which can either have a negative effect on ourselves and others or be positive and successful.

❖ Life beliefs theory

Professor Ronnie Janoff-Bulman, from the United States, in her book Shattered Assumptions, suggests that we can understand something about human nature and loss through the 'life beliefs' theory'. The basis of this is that most human beings have three fundamental beliefs which can affect how they react to life events and especially to traumatic incidents: that the world is a good place in which to live, that the world has a meaning and that 'I am a good and worthy person'.

• Invulnerability: this is the belief that the world is a benevolent place and 'I am invulnerable and will live forever'. Most of us do not think each day that we are going to have a serious accident or illness or die; we have an inbuilt defence mechanism which just lets us get on with our lives and usually expect that all will be well. This is the belief that bad things do not happen to us, they only happen to other people. It is not exactly that we think or believe that we are totally invulnerable but that we don't think about it very often and live believing that life just goes on: "I know that bad and difficult things can happen, that's life, but not to me!" The American actor and film-maker Woody Allen was asked if he was afraid of dying. Apparently he replied, 'I'm not afraid of dying. I'm just not going to be there when it happens!' I suppose that, if we bother to think about it, most of us feel like this. For some, this is a wonderful and beautiful world and we might believe that 'someone up there' is looking after us and perhaps have strong beliefs and a great deal of support from our own faith or religious community. This confidence for the future can also come from our own sense of self-worth and from the love and support of family and friends.

My wife attended the cremation of the wife of a friend. She was an atheist and wanted a wicker coffin and a Humanist committal. It was a wonderful celebration of her life. However, there was a smile at the end of the commemoration as everyone was asked to stand and sing together the old Vera Lynn song, 'We'll meet again, don't know where, don't know when, but I know we'll meet again some sunny day'. Even in death there can be life and hope that all will be well!

• Purpose: this is the belief that the world is meaningful and that life must have a purpose, even if we don't know what the purpose is. Our purpose usually includes people or things: a partner, family and friends, work, home, hobbies, our possessions and probably the cat or dog! Even if we don't know exactly what the purpose is, most of us might say that 'the purpose is to live a good life, care for others and ourselves and try to make this world a better place in which to live'.

Those who experience trauma, especially such things as rape, torture, war, being diagnosed with a terminal illness, or anything which is disastrous, devastating or violent, usually ask questions about human nature and, if the trauma is caused by human beings, wish to know why people behave like this. When I spoke to members of staff in the British Council in Nairobi, after the bombing of the US Embassy, I talked about the incident and possible traumatic reactions to it and then asked if there were any questions. The questions they wanted me to answer were not about trauma but about purpose, meaning and people. 'Why did they do this?' 'What kind of a person does something like this?' 'Are they like us?' 'Are they people with feelings and a conscience or are they just animals?' The question 'why?' is often not a practical one but more often a question about morality, about right and wrong and about human experience and behaviour.

Usually we believe that we are in charge of ourselves and our own future and that this gives some meaning and purpose to our lives. To have this control taken away can lead us to believe that life is capricious, brutal, unpredictable and cruel and that we are nothing more than pawns in the deadly game of life. This lack or loss of control can be a major factor in determining how we might react to traumatic events. I have a colleague who hates travelling in a car as a passenger, or in an aeroplane, because he doesn't like any situation in which he is not in control and, when he is not the driver or pilot, reacts with fear, shaking and nervousness, expecting the worst to happen. Traumatic experiences can create the same feelings and reactions. For some, it might be holding up our hands and screaming at the apparent injustice of life. 'Why me?' 'Why him?' 'Why us?' However, some learn to cope with the difficulties and traumas of life in their own way and come to some conclusions to which they cling and which help them to cope, no matter how illogical they might seem.

In 1964, when I served in a parish in Liverpool, there was a cultural belief that when a baby or child died there must be a purpose behind it. I recall sitting on a number of occasions with a family, usually after the funeral, when someone would say quietly but firmly, 'Well, vicar! God takes the best flowers first, doesn't he?' Everyone present would nod sympathetically. I would also nod my head slowly, even though I didn't believe it but would look at grandma, age 94, sitting in the corner, and think, 'Grandma must have been a very bad person to live so long!' Here were people trying to make some meaning and sense of a senseless event and who was I, at such a moment, to shatter the beliefs that gave them some comfort? In spite of what had happened it helped them to believe that there was a purpose in their terrible loss and, at the time, this gave them hope and the strength to carry on.

• Self-esteem: we tend to believe, generally, that we are good people, or at least as good as anyone else. 'I always try to do the right things and in a difficult situation would do my best and behave well.' When there is a traumatic event, some people react in this way but, even when we have done our best, we can still question our own abilities and think that we have failed. Also, there is what is called the fonly syndrome: 'fonly I'd done that rather than this', 'fonly I'd got there earlier', 'fonly I'd screamed and kicked him'. 'If only!' Also, following a traumatic incident, we might use words such as 'ought', 'should' and 'could'. Each of these words has its own meaning. 'Ought' can imply a sense of responsibility or even of divine imperative! 'I ought' might be the response of a police officer, doctor or other professional who expects to help people and save lives but it can apply to anyone. 'Should' implies that there is something I didn't do and 'could' implies that there was a particular course of action which was within my ability to do but, for whatever reason, I didn't do it. When traumatised, or working with the traumatised, it is sometimes helpful to challenge these words when they are used and to ask what they mean and then, if appropriate, to look at what the consequences might have been had you, or they, done what you think you ought to have done, should have done, didn't or couldn't do! These expressions of lack of self-worth and self-esteem need to be challenged.

Alan was walking along a pathway beside a river in flood when he saw three young boys playing on the opposite bank, running close to the edge and throwing sticks and stones into the water. He thought of shouting at them but decided not to and walked on. A few seconds later he heard a shout, turned around and saw that one of the boys had slipped into the river and was being swept away. He ran back but it was too late. He could do nothing other than stand there helplessly and watch. There were no ropes of lifebelts nearby and, worst of all, Alan couldn't swim. Later, he tore himself apart saying such things as: 'If only I had shouted at them when I first saw them! If only I had learned to swim I could have dived in and saved him. I could have jumped in and grabbed a log or branch and kicked my feet and dragged him to the bank.'

He was asked to look very carefully at what he was saying and to think back and work through the incident. The first questions to ask were why he had gone for a walk and why he hadn't shouted at the boys. He said that he went for a walk most evenings because he wished to relax and have some time on his own after a day's work and didn't want any hassle or stress. Because the boys were from a housing estate opposite he thought that the only response would have been foul language and rude gestures. So, he decided not to shout. The next aim was to get him to talk through the early part of the incident when he first saw the boys and to say what he was thinking at the time and not what he thought or felt about it now. As he talked about it and his feelings and making the decision not to shout, he began to see that as he couldn't have known what was going to happen and had, at that moment, made what was a rational and reasonable decision: he had his own good reasons for not shouting. When asked why he couldn't swim he said that as a child he had always been afraid of water.

At school he had told the swimming instructor and was always made to sit at the side of the pool and watch. He never learned to swim and there was a good reason for this. He was then asked to talk about what happened when he heard the shout and had to stand there helpless. He said that he should have jumped in and might have been able to grab a log or something so he was asked how he could have done this and what might have happened had he tried to do it. After agreeing to do so, Alan was then asked to close his eyes and to imagine and describe the river. He said that he could see the river quite clearly: it was in flood and rushing along carrying debris and rubbish, but he also began to see that had he jumped in he would certainly have drowned and that this would have meant that two people were dead, not just one. He said that he had realised that the river was travelling so fast that the boy had disappeared into the distance and that even if he had been running, or in a motor-boat, he would not have caught up in time to save the boy. He also acknowledged that it takes only a few minutes for someone to drown. He still felt angry, sad and guilty about what had happened but he could now see that, under the circumstances, there was nothing he could have done, that these feelings were natural and that he was not to blame. Also, when he looked at the possible consequences, he spoke about what his partner and children would have thought and gone through had he drowned.

So, the belief is that 'I'm going to live forever, the world is benevolent and meaningful and I am a person of worth'. But, if any one or more of these core beliefs is upset or challenged by what happens to us, our world, beliefs and capacity to cope can be turned upside down. The basic things we believe and accept as normal in our lives, like the boy in the river, can be swept away. Following traumatic and even devastating experiences, some people can maintain their beliefs, rise to the challenge and can cope, even finding new meaning and hope. Others might come to believe that the world is a terrible and unjust place in which to live, that life is pointless and without meaning and that the belief in our own goodness is a lie, especially when we believe that we have failed in some way. We might also come to the conclusion that we are being punished for something we have done. The shattering of these three core beliefs, or any one of them, can influence how we might react to a traumatic event.

❖ The Iceberg theory

The theory is that people are like icebergs floating in the sea where a small part of the iceberg is visible above the water. As we float around, we see other people, but we only see the visible, conscious parts of who they are. Most is hidden beneath the surface! See Figure 1.

• **The conscious mind**: about one-eighth of the iceberg is above the water and this is where we experience everything around us as we float about in the sea. We are aware of our surroundings and see and experience other people and the calmness or roughness of the sea and the weather, but we can't see anything beneath the surface. We can look at others floating around us but can't tell very much about them except what they look like, what they say and how they behave. Through our five senses, we see, hear, touch, taste, smell and experience other people on the surface and the information is fed into our brains and becomes immediately available to us. This information can be stored away in our sub-conscious or unconscious memory, while some, perhaps regarded as unimportant, might be discarded and forgotten. As we get to know people we experience more of what lies below the surface.

• **The sub-conscious**: this is just below the surface where we store our memories, some of which are instantly available to us: where you live, your name, address and telephone number, what happened this morning and yesterday or the week before when it was your birthday. Sometimes we have to think hard before the memory surfaces while at other times we just can't remember, no matter how long or how hard we try, or the memory returns later when we might not even be thinking about it. The deeper these memories, emotions, feelings, thoughts and experiences are buried, the more difficult they are to recall but this can depend on how disturbing or how powerful they were at the time. If they are happy memories, we can remember someone or something with affection and a smile. At other times we might feel sad, angry, disturbed or distressed as we recall memories of people or events and especially if they are from a difficult or traumatic incident from the past.

• **The unconscious**: deeper still is the unconscious, where memories are buried away, most of which are not immediately available to us and some which remain completely hidden:

We don't even know they are there. They can be good, bad or indifferent but sometimes they are very

Figure 1

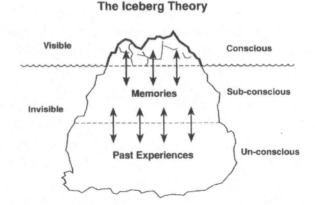

distressing, vivid or surprising.

I was visiting my parents and talking to my father. He cheered me up, as he usually did, by talking about someone from the past. 'Do you remember Harry Smith? He was at school with you'. When I replied, 'Yes', he said, as he usually did, 'He's dead! It was in the local paper!' One day he mentioned the name of a boy I had been with in primary school during the Second World War who had died. I suddenly remembered that he had a very severe speech impediment and called me 'Oiky-gokkie'. Immediately, I could see his face clearly and even hear his voice. Although I can still remember what he called me, the rest has now gone and, as I write this, I can't see what he looked like, remember his name or hear his voice. But it is somewhere there, hidden deep in my unconscious and a memory waiting for the right trigger to resurrect it.

The theory is that, whether we know it or not, experiences are pushed deep into the unconscious part of the iceberg, especially if they are uncomfortable or traumatic, and we might even believe that they have gone away. But they can be locked in the depths because we can't or don't want to remember them. This three storey model can help us to see that experiences which are buried away can, unknowingly, influence us and emerge when something on the surface triggers the memory. The memory can also come hurtling to the surface without any trigger or warning.

Think of Robert, from the car crash mentioned earlier, and his 'learned coping strategy' of repressing feelings and emotions into his unconscious so that he became unaware of them. This strategy of repressing emotions and experiences as a child determined the way he tried to cope with stress or threat throughout his adult life and resulted in feelings of isolation, problems with relationships, anger, guilt and disturbing dreams. The Iceberg Theory could help him to see that, as an adult, he had pushed difficult feelings away deep inside and that they were influencing how he reacted now when facing stressful or difficult situations. In therapy, hidden and disturbing memories can be resurrected in a safe environment and be acknowledged, hopefully, making their effect less disturbing or destructive.

❖ Transactional Analysis

The theory of transactional analysis, or TA as it is sometimes called, springs from the work of the psychiatrist Dr Eric Berne. Part of his theory is that human beings can operate in one of three modes, or 'ego states'. An 'ego state' is an inner system of emotions and feelings which motivates and relates to a certain set of behavioural patterns which are learned and internalised during our lives. Dr Berne suggested that, at any given time, we tend to operate in one or more of three modes: as child, adult or parent. The theory can throw some light on how and why we might react to a traumatic event and see that our reactions can depend on what we have learned or absorbed from our childhood and life experiences.

• The child mode

In the child mode, we usually respond to traumatic incidents in an emotional way and, like Robert after the car crash, develop a set of feelings, attitudes and behaviours which originated in our childhood and early life when we were dominated by parental and other external influences.

Depending on the style of parenting used, we might be either compliant or withdrawn and do as we are told or shrink into a shell and respond with a blank stare: alternatively, we could rebel and behave independently. Depending on what we observe and absorb we can be sad, temperamental and awkward or happy and co-operative and might carry these ways of reacting with us forever. If a parent is abusive, violent or on drugs or alcohol, we might think that this is how adults should be and, even if we don't act in a similar manner, the experience is still there and can influence our behaviour: when we meet someone who is addictive or aggressive, we are either attracted by them or indifferent and reject them. You might recall an incident where, as an adult, you have behaved in a 'childish' mode and later, reacted with feelings of frustration, anger, guilt, regret or humiliation. To realise why, how and when you are reacting like a child can help you to understand and, perhaps, accept and adjust positively to your reactions.

- The adult mode

In adult mode we tend to be more rational, capable, objective and logical and think things through carefully before we act. We are usually in this mode when we are trying to resolve a problem or sort something out cognitively.

We can be emotional but are likely to control how we feel in order to cope and to be seen to cope and, even if there is a child within us screaming to get out, we continue to be an adult and in charge. If our parents were generally angry or aggressive, we might behave in a similar way, believing that that's how adults should behave. If parents were kind and loving, attentive and supportive, we might come to the conclusion that this is how adults should be and we react accordingly.

- The parent mode

In this mode we are generally nurturing, caring and supportive. However, how we react in this mode, as with the other modes, will depend not only on how our parents behaved but on how we have interpreted their behaviour.

Parents can be loving, caring, approving and supportive or authoritative, apathetic, aggressive, uncaring and bullying. In our own parenting mode, we might act in any of these ways: we are affectionate, considerate and thoughtful or critical, superior and denigrating. This is the voice of authority learned in childhood and in our formative years from our parents and similar figures, especially the 'giants' who influenced us such as other family members, grandparents, teachers and people we have grown to respect or hate!

• Transactional analysis and trauma

At its simplest the child is our 'felt' and emotional personality, the Adult is our 'thought', our rational personality and the Parent is our Guiding or authority figure. All three are the taught and caught experiences we learn as we grow and develop and can determine how we behave and react to traumatic and other events in our lives. Knowing how and why we are reacting can help us to cope and, where necessary, perhaps change our behaviour or even the way we think and interpret events and experiences.

❖ Crisis intervention theory

Crisis intervention theory developed in the USA during and after the Second World War from civilian experiences such as the Cocoanut Grove nightclub disaster in 1942, mentioned earlier, where certain strategies for helping were advocated:

• **Early intervention**: be proactive and remove people from the stressor.
• **Relaxation and rest**: these should be encouraged as necessary.
• **Treat all reactions as normal**: do not turn people into patients who are ill.
• **Allow and encourage people to talk** – with someone they know or trust.
• **Give reassurance**, comfort and support.

The IPE systems of immediacy, proximity and expectation and crisis intervention theory use similar strategies,
which suggests that whatever the incident, whether
military or civilian, there is a common way of treating
people and helping them to cope. In the First World
War these ideas were suggested by Dr Thomas Salmon,
giving early treatment to psychological casualties near
the front line.

At the centre of crisis intervention theory is the concept
of homoeostasis, which envisages a balance between
the cognitive and emotional aspects of our response to
life events. As we grow and develop, a balance is usually
achieved between our ability to reason, think and cope
on the one hand and our emotional reactions on the
other. This balance fluctuates from moment to moment
throughout our lives. Sometimes, emotions and feelings
dominate and sometimes the opposite occurs when we
move into rational and logical mode. Either, or both, of
these can determine the way we think, how we interpret
the event and how we behave.

Like an old hanging scales weighing-machine there are
emotions and feelings on one side and rational thinking
on the other side: the scales go up and down, one way or
the other, until one side dominates, depending on the
weight and nature of reactions or experiences placed
on them. Our internal scales swing up and down as we
attempt to create a balance in our lives, especially when
something goes wrong and we feel strong emotions or
physical reactions. Each person's homoeostatic balance
is different because we are all different and respond
to different events at different times and in different
ways. I might cope well with a stressful situation and the
balance is fairly equal, but, on another occasion, even a
similar situation, the balance can be upset and I break
down and respond with anger, fear, confusion and
frustration. If our mechanisms and strategies are not

appropriate or do not work, the balance can be upset and lead to an emotional crisis.

Crisis intervention theory outlines four stages but, although the stages can be similar, these reactions do not necessarily apply to bereavement and grief.

• **Impact stage:** this takes place during and after an incident where there can be disorientation and the desire to run away or to freeze or fight any threat. Initial reactions are usually of shock and disbelief and intervention comes through allowing ventilation of emotions and reactions, hopefully reducing anxiety and distress. This stage can be as short as 36-48 hours after the event, or longer, depending on the nature and intensity of the incident and the level of reactions. Normally, therapeutic interventions should not be attempted within this period.

• Withdrawal and confusion stage: usually after a few days, people can deny that they have any reactions yet might still experience feelings of shock, detachment, confusion and unreality. Help is offered by considering what resources are available and acceptable, especially talking about the experience through counselling or some form of therapy.

• Adjustment stage: in the third stage, emotional and other reactions are usually acknowledged and begin to reduce in impact and effect. This can begin after a month or so, and there might even be positive feelings of hope.

• Reconstruction stage: information is offered about resources available for helping and support and there can be a growth in confidence and in positive thinking about one's self and the future. Life begins to move on: 'I haven't forgotten what happened and how I reacted, but I am gradually learning to cope.'

The aim of treatment is to restore the cognitive-emotive homeostatic balance and, if the right kind of treatment is offered and is successful, the balance can be restored and the individual will recover. Dr Gerald Caplan believed that this can usually be achieved for most people within four to five weeks, which is the time when, if certain reactions continue or intensify, PTSD can be diagnosed.

❖ Independents and Klingons

This theory is based on concepts of projection and identification and is adapted from the work of the psychoanalyst Lily Pincus in her book on bereavement, Death and the Family. She believed that, within a wide spectrum, people can be put into one of two basic groups: the 'Independents' generally gravitate to one end and those I call the 'Klingons' to the other.

• The Independents

Lily Pincus believed that those who have high self-esteem and a positive self-image tend to cope better with loss and bereavement than those who have 'clinging' personalities; this can also apply to coping with trauma. These are individuals who can cope well on their own and, although they might have partners, families and friends, they do not 'cling' to them and are not 'needy'. In early life the 'independents' probably had a supportive and positive upbringing and developed a strong feeling of being loved and cared for. They would say, 'I am loved for what I am' and they have a belief in themselves and in their own abilities without being arrogant or self-centred. When they meet other people, or fall in love, they do not cling to them or become totally dependent on them. Although they love no less than others, they usually have their own interests and hobbies and do not need to do everything together. When they are bereaved, they usually say 'something has been taken from my life and I feel empty inside'. They survive well because their inner sense of self-worth is not wholly dependent on something or someone external. These 'independents' would probably be the survivors in the psychiatrist Bruno Bettelheim's book The Informed Heart, about living and coping in Nazi concentration camps. They had a positive sense of their own identity and a very strong purpose in life, usually political or religious, which gave them the strength to carry on.

• **The Klingons**

The Klingons are people who desperately need someone or something to which they can attach themselves in order to boost their sense of self-esteem and self-worth: they need others in order to be themselves. It is possible that in early life, because of the way they were treated, they came to see themselves as unloved or even unlovable and of little worth. In response to this background, Klingons tend to cling desperately to somebody or something, even an object or a pet, which they 'clasp to their bosom' and depend on. In early life, they were probably unable to develop a positive sense of being separate and having a sense of their own identity, and any identity they did have would be dependent upon someone or something else. They would say, 'Without you, I am nothing!'

The point is that the clinging is not just to something which is external but because they internalise the person or object and this becomes part of who and what they are. When they are bereaved, unlike the 'independents' who says, 'something has been taken from me and I feel empty', they tend to say 'something has died and is dead inside me!' A good example of 'Klingons' can be found in the old TV series, 'Ever Decreasing Circles', about a young married couple whose neighbours, Howard and Hilda, live out their lives through and in each other. When Howard goes to work in the morning it is like a major bereavement. Hilda stands, almost in tears while

Howard reluctantly drags himself away and leaves for work, looking back at her as though he might never see her again. They are into 'his and hers' clothing, wearing identical jumpers and sweaters, and are also inseparable, doing everything together.

After I left the army I was involved with others who had also left, some of whom couldn't adjust or cope and were going through trauma and a terrible sense of loss. The 'copers' tended to be people who were 'Independents' while, generally, those who couldn't cope were 'Klingons'. This ability to cope, or not was, I believe, related to the nature of their relationship with their work: the army was everything and had been totally absorbed! Alan was a typical example of a 'Klingon'.

Alan telephoned me saying that he couldn't settle down in civilian life, was suffering from anxiety, anger, sleeplessness, disillusion, confusion and depression. He felt isolated and desperately missed the army. Life now seemed to have no meaning or purpose and he could see no future. The army, and every aspect of it, was his entire life: he had completely internalised the whole military culture and it was still there inside him, but dead. This can also apply to anyone, military or civilian, who retires, loses their job or experiences a major life change, trauma, crisis or loss. Some of these will be 'Klingons'.

It is not possible to say exactly how an 'Independent' or a 'Klingon' would react to a traumatic experience, but the 'Independents' will probably cope better because of their strength of personality, ability to cope on their own and sense of self-worth. Also, the 'Independents' have not internalised the person or object of their affections and become totally dependent upon them. However, the distinction between 'Independents' and 'Klingons' is a generalisation because they lie at each end of a wide spectrum of behaviour where most of us are moving around somewhere in between, just getting on with our lives and trying to cope with the many changes we face each day.

Bereavement and grief

Bereavement is a traumatic experience and grief can develop into symptoms of PTSD. Following a bereavement, it can take many years before some will feel that life can move on, but the pain of grief and loss can remain and return at various times and at differing levels of distress. Some will say: 'It takes time but you will get over it eventually!'

This is probably one of the most unhelpful and, sometimes, hurtful, things you can say to someone who is grieving. Most people will say: 'You do not get over it. You go through it.'

There is a three-stage model of grieving known as the SAD model of shock, anger and depression, which some might find helpful, with certain reservations. The model should also include, Recovery, which does not mean that everything is forgotten and over. Some would say: 'You never "recover"; you just learn to live with it.'

Different people will have different ways of reacting and coping and symptoms might not occur in the order outlined. This model is similar to the normal reactions of almost anyone experiencing a traumatic event: the initial shock, the emotional responses and the road to recovery.

• Shock

As with any traumatic experience the first reaction is usually one of shock with a numbing of emotions and acute feelings of emptiness. This is a natural way of reacting and surviving: the shock can enable some people to cope with the initial emotional and physical impact. Also, the many practical things which need to be done following a death can delay grieving. The presence of family and friends usually helps but these people can 'fade away' when the funeral is over and some might have little or no further contact. There can be a denial of having any reactions with feelings of unreality and thinking that it hasn't happened. The realisation that it is true might not come until after the funeral and sometimes at a much later stage. In terms of the 'Flight, Fight or Freeze' response, some will react with hysteria and panic, while others will cry and be in deep distress or feel numb, frozen and stunned. But some will react with remarkable composure.

Mary's husband Bill, who was serving in the army, was killed in a traffic accident on his way home from work. The families' officer and I, as the chaplain from the unit who knew Mary well, went to tell her and knocked on the door. Mary opened the door and invited us in. I asked her to sit down and told her what had happened. There was a brief moment of silence while Mary nodded her head. She stood up and said, 'Now, would you like tea or coffee and a biscuit? Padre, I think you take milk but no sugar.' She went into the kitchen and the families' officer whispered, 'Do you think she heard?' I said that she had heard and that this was not an unusual reaction. We all had tea and biscuits while Mary chatted about Bill leaving for work that morning and what they had been doing over the week-end. Initially, Mary reacted as though nothing had happened and it was not until after the funeral that she broke down and cried.

• Anger

Anger, representing many distressing or devastating emotional reactions, is a typical and powerful response to trauma and loss, not only anger at the loss of the loved-one but wanting an answer and asking why such things happen. Some will blame God, fate or the unfairness of life or direct the blame at something or someone else. As mentioned earlier, some might react as 'Independents' or 'Klingons': someone has been taken from them and they feel empty inside or they feel something is dead inside them. There can also be feelings of panic, self-blame, bitterness, loneliness, isolation, anxiety and fear for the future. Some will search for their loved-one and believe that they have seen him or her in the street or at home and felt their presence.

It is not unusual, during the night or in the morning, to see the person who has died standing at the bottom of the bed saying that all is well. This experience can also come much later in the grieving process and might be comforting and consoling or frightening, but it is quite normal. However, the absence of the loved-one, especially their physical presence, is devastating and things in the home are constant reminders of the loss. A particular chair or any such object, photographs or personal belongings, a smell or clothes, can bring back memories and might be comforting or upsetting, or both at the same time.

• Depression

The sensation and feelings of depression, or feeling 'down', are common: 'What's the point of carrying on? I feel so terrible and life now seems so meaningless and without purpose.'

There can also be a reduced sense of self-worth and feelings of having been abandoned:

'Why did he go like that and leave me all on my own? Part of me died with him and has left an aching hole deep inside me. I feel as though my insides have been scraped out!'

One woman, when told that it must be terrible to not have someone to do something with replied, 'It is even worse not to have someone to do nothing with!'

Some will say they have a terrible, dead 'lump' inside their throat, chest or stomach. Loss of identity is also natural, particularly when someone's status is high or their position has often been identified with the person who has died:

> We always went everywhere together and were invited out together but all that has gone now. I am on my own, nobody wants to know me and I am an embarrassment to others. Some even cross the street to avoid me when they see me. Sometimes when I meet people I know, they never mention Colin. It's as though he never existed.

This model might help some to understand their reactions but it is not quite as straightforward as this.

At the beginning of a seminar on bereavement and grief a woman on the course said that she had heard a lecturer on another course she had attended say that grief takes time and that the initial shock lasts about six months, the emotional stage about another six months, followed by another year or so of depression, but that after about two years people begin to move on!

This is based on the SAD model and might be the experience of some, but this is not how it is for most people.

• Reactions to bereavement, like other traumatic effects, can change from day to day: one day you feel devastated and can't stop crying, the next day you wake up feeling much better but later in the day the mood changes to depression and sadness. The next day you feel lost and helpless and don't know how you are going to cope but the following day you feel angry and cheated. You might then have a few days when you feel calm and a sense of peace but then you begin to feel guilty and the grief returns with a vengeance. And so it goes on. This is how most people experience grief but it is not the same for everyone. What is generally true is that however you react, this is natural for you, no matter what others might say or think.

• In order to learn to cope, as with other traumatic reactions, it is usually better to face any emotions and feelings rather than to push them down into the iceberg of your memory where you think they have gone away and believe that it is better if they are denied. However, some will choose not to talk about feelings or emotions or to face them and this should be respected, but denying reactions might result in deeper problems where some people develop what is usually called 'complicated grief'. For most people, talking helps, especially talking about the one who has died and making them live again in their life and memory. As with trauma, 'integration' of the memories can be crucial to positively surviving the loss and grief.

• Perhaps the most difficult thing to understand or accept is that the pain of grief has within it the seeds of renewal and healing. If we allow ourselves to gradually experience and feel the pain and the many different and complex feelings and reactions generated, no matter how painful or distressing, we can come through the experience to some kind of healing and renewal. It is in the very act of mourning that healing can take place. But the experience of most people is that the pain never completely goes away and, even many years later, some will say:

> You don't get over it: you go through it and learn to live with it. The pain might get easier but it is still there, waiting to come to the surface and you never know when. The slightest thing can start me off again. I cried yesterday when I saw somebody in the street I thought was him.

The same can be said for other traumatic experiences and reactions and for those suffering from stress, PTS and PTSD where reactions can vary from moment to moment and from day to day.

❖ Pessimists, optimists and trauma

Do optimists cope with trauma better than pessimists? People can interpret the same, or similar, experiences in different ways and this might depend on whether or not they are pessimists or optimists. The clue might lie in the old chestnut question, 'Is the glass of water half-full or half-empty?' It depends on how you interpret it! There is a belief by some which suggests that those who are optimists cope better with traumatic experiences than pessimists but this can be too simple. The optimist could have had negative experiences in his upbringing and life and been determined to make life better for himself and others, while the pessimist could have responded to a positive upbringing with cynicism, bitterness and anger.

• Remembering the 'life beliefs' theory', optimists might react to a traumatic event by having their positive beliefs in the goodness of the world and in their capacity to cope completely shattered. If their positive beliefs are challenged and damaged when something dreadful happens, optimists might be more vulnerable to the power of negative reactions. Also, a pessimist might cope better because they believe that life is pointless: 'I told you so! Life is without meaning, awful, nasty and short. You just have to get on with it, whatever happens. That's life!'

• Alternatively, a positive experience, perhaps receiving love and affection from another person, or from the friendship of others, might turn a pessimist into an optimist when he or she realises that life and people can be good. As with a cognitive approach, it all can depend on how you interpret a traumatic experience.

There are many similarities in these models and perhaps some of them can help our understanding of why and how someone might react to any traumatic event. They can also give some clues about what can be done about it and which treatment to offer those who suffer. The basics are: identify when there is a problem; offer help and be proactive; make people feel safe; do not treat them as 'patients' who are ill; give reassurance about the normality of their reactions; offer support; explain the availability of resources for helping and ensure on-going monitoring. When offering treatment look for the appropriate therapy: the same method and approach does not work for everybody; respect people's views and wishes; where possible, encourage people to talk about what has happened and why and how it has affected them. As for being a pessimist or an optimist, some researchers say that it is written in your genes!

Chapter 7

DEFUSING AND DEBRIEFING

Following traumatic experiences, 'Defusing', 'Critical Incident Stress Debriefing' and 'Psychological Debriefing' techniques have been used since the mid-1980s in the USA, Scandinavia and many other countries. These methods of helping came to the UK in the late 1980s and have been used after war and combat and traumatic events such as natural and man-made disasters, traffic accidents, fatal shootings, muggings, rape, aid-agency work, terrorist bombings, hostage situations, murder and armed robberies. They are recommended for use in a group sessions, although the structures are sometimes adapted and used within therapy sessions with individuals and couples.

❖ Defusing

In most organisations, such as the emergency services and the military, immediately after every major operation or incident there is usually a meeting for those involved called an operational debriefing. The senior person present gives a short talk to the group, largely about practical matters, sometimes with questions and discussion, but it would not usually include anything about psychological or emotional reactions, except perhaps, to say that any reactions are natural and normal and that help is available.

• Dr Jeffrey Mitchell's Defusing Model

In the USA, the psychologist Dr Jeffrey Mitchell, a former fire-fighter and paramedic working with the fire service in Maryland, found that at operational debriefings the availability of channels for help and support was rarely mentioned and even when it was, generally, nobody self-referred or sought help, so he devised a simple procedure which he called 'defusing'. There are three basic stages in defusing: **Introduction**, **Exploration** and **Information**. The defusing can take place shortly after an incident, or even immediately afterwards, and should last no more than an hour. It is usually informal and can be as simple as getting those involved together, explaining that this is not an investigation, allowing people to talk about their involvement in the incident, explaining about the possibility of psychological reactions and then outlining what resources are available for helping, should they be needed. The Defusing can also give an indication as to how people have coped and reacted and whether or not a longer debriefing might be needed.

❖ Debriefing

Debriefing, sometimes known as 'critical incident stress debriefing', 'critical incident debriefing' or 'psychological debriefing', is a procedure sometimes conducted after a defusing or following an incident: usually two to three days later. There are various models of debriefing, but they all have similar aims:

- Talk through what happened and help to normalise reactions.
- Enable the processing of experiences.
- Develop an element of control over reactions.
- Renew personal or group confidence and solidarity.
- Give reassurance about present and possible future reactions.
- Give information about resources for helping.

Debriefing can reduce tension and concern about reactions but, although the basic listening skills of counselling are used, usually with reframing skills, debriefing is not counselling or an injection against PTSD. Some researchers have made the mistake of assuming that the main aim of debriefing is to prevent the development of PTSD and, because of this, have come to the wrong conclusions.

- **Dr Atlé Dyregrov's psychological debriefing model**

Dr Atlé Dyregrov, a psychologist at the University of Bergen in Norway, developed his model in the 1980s and called it 'psychological debriefing'. The structure is in seven stages:

- **Introduction:** where necessary, a self and group introduction is given, an explanation of the process of debriefing is outlined and the rules about such things as confidentiality and allowing personal space for responding are agreed.
- **Expectations and Facts:** what was happening and what did you expect before the incident occurred and what happened during the incident?
- **Thoughts and sensory impressions:** what were your thoughts in the beginning and during the incident, what did you do and why and what sensory reactions and impressions did you experience?
- **Emotional reactions:** how did you feel in the beginning and later? What was the worst thing for you and how do you feel now after the event?
- **Normalisation:** the debriefer explains responses mentioned in the debriefing and gives reassurance about the normality of any reactions.
- **Future planning and coping:** what help or support is needed, if any, and what have you learned from this experience and the debriefing?

- **Disengagement**: are there any questions, giving hand-outs, thanking people for attending and final statements or comments from participants.

Where possible and appropriate, there would be monitoring of personnel and follow-up at a later date.

I used this model with groups, including after the Manchester Prison riots and with the War Grave's Registration Team, but eventually experience led me to adapt the structure of the model and this came about partly following a fatal stabbing in the north-east of England.

- ## The Middlesbrough stabbing – 1994

On 28 March 1994, a tragedy occurred in Middlesbrough, on Teesside, when a man entered Hall Garth Community College with a knife and killed a student. A few days later I heard the college head on the radio being asked what help they had been given. He said that someone came to speak to people and began by asking them about what was happening before the event occurred, to describe in detail the facts about what had happened during the incident and to say how they were feeling at the time. They were then asked to say what had happened after the incident, how they were feeling now and about the future and outlined what resources were available for helping should they be needed. It was clear that this person had used a structure similar to Dyregrov's model but which could be translated into three stages of 'before, during and after' and, from my own experience, including a 'facts, feelings and future' element: what was happening before the incident, what happened during the incident, how has it affected you and what do you need? This model included an introduction, the three main stages, using cognitive reframing techniques, and an ending.

Eventually, because of experience in using the model

in debriefing and counselling, the 'facts and feelings' stages were eventually incorporated together so that emotional and physical reactions were not completely separated but were addressed as and when they arose in telling the story and, where possible, were firmly located in the event. This technique would hope to make it clear that their reactions were normal and that it was the person or the incident which caused the physical and emotional reactions and that they were not to blame.

• Armed robbery

An armed robbery was taking place in a small branch of a building society but the manager was unaware of it because it was a very old building with very thick walls and doors and he was interviewing a couple in his office about a mortgage. The robbery took place in seconds after which one of the cashiers dashed into the manager's office shouting 'we've been robbed!' The manager just sat there, looked at the young woman, smiled and said, 'It's not April Fools' Day is it?' Three days later the debriefing took place and in discussion with the manager before the debriefing he mentioned what had happened and said that he was angry with himself and felt guilty for the way he had reacted. At one point during the debriefing a great deal of anger was expressed by members of staff at the dismissive attitude of the manager. When the young woman who had dashed into the office said that she had been upset and was very angry when the manager thought that it was a joke, I asked the manager if he would like to say anything. He looked a bit embarrassed but said that he was appalled by the way he had acted and felt terribly guilty and angry. Because of the thick and heavy doors he had not heard anything and had thought that they were playing a trick on him. He then explained that he had not said anything at the time because he felt he had to remain strong in order to deal with the aftermath of the robbery and help members of staff. He also said that, when at home with his family that evening, he had cried and felt ashamed about the way he had reacted. He said that he couldn't sleep very well and wanted to say to everyone that he was sorry. There was silence for a moment and then the response of his staff was electric: everybody began to say that he should not feel ashamed or guilty and that his reactions were understandable. There was a tremendous feeling in the group of support for one another, especially for the manager.

At the end of the debriefing all said that they felt much better about what had happened and that a great deal of tension and anxiety had been defused. They felt more confident about themselves, about others in the team and also believed that they were much stronger as a group. Afterwards, the manager said that the debriefing had made such a difference to him and to the members of staff. It had given him an opportunity to say how he had felt at the time and to apologise. He was proud by the way his staff had responded and supported him.

- Self-debriefing

It is possible to conduct a self-debriefing. A man who was severely injured in a railway accident where there were many fatalities was told that he might never walk or work again. He said that a visitor had brought him my book Critical Incident Debriefing and that this had saved his life! Using the model in the book, he had debriefed himself in hospital and this gave him confidence and reassurance and had helped his recovery. The following is a personal experience and, although a minor incident, it caused me some distress and anger.

I drove into town and went into a shop to have a holiday film developed and asked the assistant for the one-hour service. Because they were having problems with the equipment he asked me to return in two hours.

I duly returned and was billed for the one-hour service. When I questioned this he replied that it was not his fault so I said, very politely, that I would not pay for the one hour service. He was very angry and shouted at me, demanding the money. I controlled my anger, but he became increasingly rude and aggressive, turned his back on me, and walked away. I was steaming with frustration and anger so asked another member of staff for the manager. The manager arrived, apologised, and asked me to pay for the cheaper two-hour service. I left the shop shaking, breathing quickly and heavily, with my heart pounding. I walked back to my car, sat inside and decided to debrief myself. I began by controlling my breathing and, using the 'before, during and after' process, worked my way through the incident in detail outlining my feelings and reactions from leaving home to returning to the car. It took about half an hour but I felt much better: my breathing was back to normal, my heart had stopped pounding and I began to laugh. I felt calmer and the anger had turned into humour.

- **Debriefing after extended experiences of trauma**

Using the model in two sessions, the following is an example of debriefing a young man who worked for an aid-agency.

Ian had worked for a small aid agency in an east European country where he was taken and held hostage for five weeks. He arranged to come to see me but decided to go on holiday abroad first. On his return he called and said that he urgently needed someone to talk to so we arranged to meet. He said that while on holiday he had been irritable and frightened, had intrusive thoughts and nightmares and felt 'paranoid'. He had served in the British army but left to work for an aid agency because his experience as a soldier had convinced him of the need to help people who were suffering in countries where there was war and conflict.

He went overseas as one of three aid workers but was totally unprepared for what he found. Shortly after arriving, while travelling in a Land Rover, he and his colleagues were stopped by an armed group of civilians who forced them all, at gunpoint, to look at the bodies of men, women and children who had been shot and mutilated. Ian said that he immediately felt detached and withdrawn from the whole scene and had an 'out-of-body experience' where he was watching himself from above. This happened a number of times where he was forced, at gunpoint, to view bodies after atrocities. Two weeks later he was travelling in a vehicle with two companions when they were stopped again by armed men wearing balaclava-type masks. They were bundled into a van and taken away as hostages. He said that he never knew who the men were or why they had been taken hostage; they were threatening and frequently waving weapons at them. Although they were not beaten or tortured, there was a constant physical threat against them and they were afraid that they might be shot or beheaded. During the five weeks, the place where they were staying was shelled and mortared, which he described as 'terrifying'. On his release and return home his reactions were of horror and fear and he suffered from nightmares, flash-backs, irritation, anger and intrusive images, especially of dead bodies. All this was outlined in the first session, where he became upset and angry while telling the story and describing his emotional and physical reactions. He talked about his expectations before he went abroad and about his feelings of being terrified and powerless, but realised that he and his companions could do nothing: they were totally helpless. At the end of the first session he said that he had found it useful to talk through his experiences and he felt more comfortable, optimistic and positive about his reactions. This session had taken over two hours and, because of his other commitments, it was three months before I saw him again. He arrived, looking very fit and well and said that the first session had helped him and he believed that his reactions had been significantly reduced. He still had flash-backs and had been upset by Guy Fawkes' Day fireworks where the flashes and bangs had disturbed him. He still had dreams about being held hostage but dreams where all the ruined buildings had been restored and there was a feeling of peace. He was calmly showing his friends the places where he had been and said that he saw the dreams as signs of a positive recovery. When he first returned from being held hostage, he had talked to his friends endlessly about what he had been through. However, when they asked him about what had happened, he said that their eyes gradually glazed over. He had felt like an outsider but now realised that they could never know or understand what he had been through. He thought that his dreams of showing them around were because of his desire for them to know where he had been and what he had experienced and that the restored building and sense of peace reflected his present feelings. A few weeks after our second session, he telephoned to say that he was now working for an organisation which helped hostages and their families and felt that he was now coping well and that this, for him, was a very positive move.

❖ The debriefing controversy

Much controversy has been caused by debriefing procedures, largely because some influential researchers have claimed that debriefing does not work, can make people worse and does not prevent the development of PTSD. However, the two most influential pieces of research used to debunk debriefing were not conducted using 'proper' debriefing techniques. They ignored certain key protocols laid down by Mitchell and Dyregrov, the founders of this technique. In one influential piece of research into Debriefing burns victims, some debriefees were still suffering physically, some sessions were as short as forty minutes and conducted by nurses trained in a morning. In another piece of research, a team conducted Debriefings with road traffic victims and used one hour sessions because that's what they normally used in their other therapeutic work.

These two pieces of research were flawed and were not classed by Dyregrov as proper debriefings because they did not fit the required criteria. Also, many professionals consider it unwise to conduct therapy with people when they are still suffering physically and that nurses could not be trained in one morning to conduct debriefing sessions. I ran a two-day course on psychological debriefing at Bristol University for ten years. These courses were only for professionally trained therapists, counsellors or psychologists and the shortest debriefing I have done with an individual took just under two hours. In the first forty minutes of any debriefing I will have just begun to get to know something about the debriefee or debriefees and the incident.

One important point is that it was wrongly assumed by these researchers that debriefing was designed as an antidote to the development of PTSD and this meant that their work led to wrong conclusions. In the early years of psychological debriefing it was hoped by some that debriefing might have a positive influence on reducing the possibility of the development of acute or severe symptoms, but it was never designed with the aim of preventing PTSD. Dr Atlé Dyregrov described this kind of research as more a study of 'bad quality crisis intervention' than of debriefing and said that the methodology of some researchers did not support their conclusions.

The National Institute for Clinical Excellence (NICE) in the UK has issued guidelines which decree that debriefing should not be used as a one-off, single session intervention but that 'trauma focused psychological treatment' – cognitive behavioural therapy or eye movement desensitising and reprocessing, both described in the next chapter – should be offered. They also suggest that where symptoms of PTSD are mild and have been present fewer than four weeks, 'watchful waiting' should be used. This 'watchful waiting' is in line with the diagnostic criteria for PTSD, which is not usually given as a diagnosis until after a month. Both Mitchell and Dyregrov stress that debriefing should normally be used as a group process and as part of a 'crisis intervention programme' which should include pre-incident education of all personnel about the normality of any reactions, facilities for support, on-going monitoring and facilities for referral.

I have used psychological debriefing and defusing techniques for almost twenty-five years and have found that debriefing and cognitive reframing skills can be used with individuals and groups with success and that these skills can be incorporated into other counselling and therapy sessions. However, in helping those who suffer from traumatic-stress reactions, there is no method which cures all ills. Some methods and techniques, such as cognitive reframing skills, work for some but not for others. Some have found the right therapy for them in looking after horses while, for others, it is gardening or painting or helping others! But more about cognitive techniques and treatment in the next chapter.

Chapter 8

TRAUMA AND TREATMENT

A very wide range of treatments are offered for PTS and PTSD. They provide not only therapy, but also the theories behind them, which can also help in understanding why and how we might react to traumatic events.

❖ The IPE (PIE) system

Treatment during the First World War has already been mentioned and, from this conflict, there emerged a system for the treatment of traumatised combatants which eventually became known as the 'IPE' or 'PIE' system, mentioned earlier. This system was developed in the armed forces, for coping and for the treatment of those who were traumatised. It is similar in structure to a number of other approaches to treatments and theories mentioned in Chapters, 6, 7 and 8 and has three suggested stages.

• **Immediacy**: do not wait but be proactive and do something immediately: when symptoms are recognised, those affected should be removed from the stressor. This implies the importance of education and understanding for all concerned so that they can recognise symptoms, react appropriately and have resources and facilities available for support, referral and treatment. Because shock, denial and suppression of emotions are typical reactions to trauma, it might be difficult for a sufferer to ask for help but when symptoms are recognised and someone is in distress, the correct procedure is to take immediate action to help them.

• **Proximity:** It is important to keep the individual as near to their comrades as possible. In the army, in the First and Second World Wars, this would be in the regimental aid post, or equivalent, near the front-line, where the soldier would probably know the regimental medical officer, chaplain and medical orderlies and even the bandsmen who would be acting as stretcher-bearers.

Also, some regiments in the First World War were 'Pals' battalions, consisting of men who had joined up from the same village, factory or town and had probably gone to school and worked together, so many of them would know each other. Most importantly, unless physically injured, the individual should not be put into hospital because this would suggest that he is 'ill' and would become a 'patient in pyjamas' who might never recover. Some believe that in the First World War many who were sent back to the UK and put into hospital either took longer to recover or never recovered. Sadly, on some occasions, men who were removed from their regiments for treatment, on recovering, were sent to a different regiment where they didn't know anyone. This made it more difficult for them to cope and in some cases it exacerbated reactions, hence the need to keep them in a familiar environment with familiar people. At the outbreak of the Second World War, approximately 120,000 people were receiving pensions for psychological problems from the First World War.

• **Expectation:** reactions should be seen, by all involved, as 'normal' and 'natural' and the condition one of being 'temporarily indisposed'; the message is that 'given time you will recover'. With physical comfort, reassurance and support the individual should fairly soon be back on duty with his comrades. Remember the reactions of the blind soldier to the comforting and reassuring words of Captain Winters in Band of Brothers, mentioned earlier. In this case, reassurance and a few kind and supportive words were enough to elicit a 'cure'.

The IPE system was used in the First World War by Dr Charles Myers, who suggested treating people near to the front line. This three-stage model was resurrected again in the Second World War and is now used generally as the basis for the treatment of psychological casualties in the military: react immediately and make them safe, keep them with familiar people and give them comfort and reassurance.

In 1980, after PTSD was included in the American psychiatrist's manual, the DSM, the British army produced a seven-stage list of principles taught to officers for coping with 'battle-shock', principles which were in line with the IPE/PIE system. These principles are for all military personnel, not just soldiers. For 'him' we include 'her'.

- **Prevent evacuation of the soldier** to increase the likelihood of recovery.
- **Staff and the soldier** are to have the expectation that he will recover.
- **Treat him as a soldier** and not as someone who is ill.
- **Offer rest and sleep** but, unless necessary, no alcohol or medication.
- **Encourage him to talk** to someone he knows and trusts – if possible, someone from his own regiment or unit.
- **Give him something to do** – if he is physically able.
- **Keep him in touch with his unit** so that he knows what is happening to his comrades and that he and they can expect him to return to duty.

In this instruction, the soldier was to be treated within his unit in the first two days and then, if necessary, moved to a rehabilitation unit for up to six days. For those who do not recover, there would be evacuation to a unit where there were military professionals such as psychiatrists and psychiatric nurses. There was no list or explanation of possible reactions but the document said that if this system was used, approximately 90 per cent of soldiers would recover within four days. In 1980, bearing in mind the present and future attitudes towards stress and trauma within the military, this document seems to have had little effect on personnel or procedures.

❖ Cognitive behavioural therapy

One important development in understanding reactions and the treatment of PTS and PTSD is the use of cognitive behavioural therapy, usually referred to as CBT.

At its simplest, CBT is based on the belief that if we can change the way we think, it can change the way we feel and react to events. It is a process encouraging people to look at their experiences and reactions in a cognitive way by using techniques such as 'reframing': seeing and reviewing the event in a new way and looking at it from a different point of view or standing outside the event and looking in as an observer. CBT attempts to re-establish the 'homeostatic' balance, the balance between what we think, the cognitive, and what we feel, the emotive parts of our nature. During and after a traumatic event an individual can be overwhelmed by emotions and feelings: the facts of what happened can fade into the background and the normal, internal 'cognitive-emotive balance', can be challenged and upset. Disturbance of this balance can contribute to the development of feelings such as self-blame, anger, shame, fear, loss of self-esteem, guilt, survivor-guilt, and feelings of inadequacy and helplessness. As mentioned earlier, words and expressions such as "I could have, should have, ought to" might be used by sufferers and the 'if only' syndrome can result in taking responsibility for what has happened, even when you are blameless and have done your best. 'Reframing' can challenge you to look at the experience and reactions to it in a different way. The way you think can change and this might change the way you feel.

• Figure 2 . What can you see? Can you see any people, objects, animals, faces? Spend a few minutes looking at it trying to make some sense of it. Then turn to Figure 3 to see either how right you were or what it really is. When people are traumatised they often try to make sense of the experience. 'Reframing' can help them to look at the way they have interpreted the event and to see that they have come to the wrong conclusions – e.g. they feel guilty when, in fact, they did nothing wrong or they did their best.

It is not unusual for people to interpret experiences, especially when disturbing or traumatic, in terms of their feelings rather than what actually happened or is happening to them. 'I shouldn't have reacted like this!' 'I could have done something but just stood there frozen with fear. What's wrong with me? I must be stupid and pathetic!' These feelings don't take into account the nature of the event and our natural or normal reactions to it. Also, human emotional reactions such as fear, anger and guilt are normal and necessary: if we were never frightened, we might put ourselves and others in more danger; when faced with a threat, it is normal to respond with a freeze, fight or flight reaction. If we are never angry, nothing in the world which is unjust or wrong will be challenged or changed; if we never feel guilty or ashamed we won't acknowledge our responsibility for something we have done wrong. The problem is that when we are traumatised we can feel these emotions when there is nothing to fear or to be angry, guilty or ashamed about. Reframing aims to correct the balance. But this is not a new approach. The first century Greek Stoic philosopher Epictetus, sometimes referred to as 'The Father of CBT, said: 'People are disturbed not so much by events as by the views which they take of them'.

Shakespeare wrote in *Hamlet*: 'There is neither good nor bad, but thinking makes it so.'

Bruno Bettelheim, the Austrian psychiatrist who survived two concentration camps under the Nazis, records in his book *The Informed Heart* that he was surprised to find that those he would normally have regarded as neurotic, such as people with very strong religious or political beliefs, seemed to cope better than those who had no such beliefs: what we believe and think can influence how we cope. In other words, our response to an incident will partly depend on how we interpret it. This can help us to re-assess and understand our experiences in a different light and enable us to move towards integrating them into their lives.

❖ Cognitive reframing

Cognitive reframing is a technique and skill used in CBT which can also be used in counselling and other kinds of therapy. It can help an individual, or group, to explore their involvement in a traumatic incident and encourage them to reinterpret their reactions to it and see them in a different way. While firmly acknowledging the reality of emotional reactions, it can change what they think, believe and feel.

A Cognitive reframing model

Reframing can help by doing four things:

- **Locate**

Firmly locate any emotional or physical reactions and place them where they were triggered in the event or experience. This can help people to realise that what they are feeling and thinking is the result of what happened in the incident rather than due to any fault or weakness of their own. We usually only have feelings because something, or someone, external has triggered that feeling or emotion. If you attack me or attempt to harm me I can be frightened, feel threatened and either run away, freeze with shock or fight back. I can still feel the fear afterwards, and this fear is generated by me, but would be the direct result of the attack by you and not because I am pathetic or to blame: 'I did not ask for this to happen. You (or this experience) did it to me.'

- **Challenge**

Challenge irrational or illogical beliefs, feelings, assumptions and statements, especially use of the words 'ought', 'should', 'could' and 'if only'. It is easy to beat yourself to death with your feelings and emotions but 'reframing' can help you to see and understand why such words need to be challenged. Experiencing reactions is natural but responses can be the result of wrong thinking. You might come to the conclusion that you did not do what you could have done at the time and that you have failed. You feel guilty and ashamed but when you are led to challenge these beliefs you discover by cognitively reframing the event that you did everything you could at the time and, even if you still feel guilty, you are not to blame.

- **Ask direct questions**

Ask questions to put the person into the event and encourage them to explore what happened and how and why they were involved. Questions should be linked to the facts of the event and should be asked in a non-judgemental and non-critical but direct manner. Thinking of the man who couldn't swim and the drowning boy mentioned earlier, questions could be:

- Why did you go for a walk beside the river - what were you thinking or feeling?
- What did you think when you first saw the boys on the river bank?
- What thoughts came into your mind when you heard the shout?
- What were your reasons, at the time, for not shouting?
- Describe the river: what was it like and how fast was it going?
- How far away was the boy when you ran towards him?
- You said that you couldn't swim. Is there a reason for this?
- If you had jumped into the rushing water and that you can't swim, how long would it have taken you to get to the boy and what were your chances of surviving?
- How would your partner and family have reacted if you had drowned?

These kinds of questions could be asked within the context of the therapy or counselling session at appropriate points.

- **Discuss possible consequences**

Ask questions about and discuss the possible or likely consequences of any actions. In the case of the man who couldn't swim, it would help to look at the word 'ought' and discover that, in terms of 'I ought to have jumped into the water and rescued him', there would have been consequences. Through reframing, he could say: 'I realise now that if I had jumped in I would have drowned!'

Also, because of the speed and state of the river, and the distance the boy was from him he could not have reached him in time, and it takes only a few minutes for someone to drown.

These four stages of cognitive reframing can be included in a counselling or therapy session. The following are examples of reframing.

Figure 3
Cowboy on a horse

Go back to Figure 2 and see if you can now see the cowboy on a horse. If not – return to Figure 3 and try again!

• **Armed robbery – 1994**

In 1994, many building societies and banks had a fairly open system of counters without the security glass and protection usually found today.

Peter, age 22, was sitting as a cashier beside two

young women colleagues, all at separate desks. A man entered the branch wearing a long coat and stood near to the door until the branch was empty of customers. He approached Peter, produced a sawn-off shotgun, pushed it into Peter's face, used some rather nasty words, and aggressively ordered Peter to give him the cash. Peter went into shock but managed to carry out the procedure he was trained to do in such circumstances: don't panic, try to stay calm and give him the money. When the robber had left, Peter was so ashamed of what he had done that he ran into the toilets and was so frightened that he wet himself.

After the group debriefing, Peter said that he wanted to talk to me on his own and, when we were alone, said that he was not sleeping, felt guilty and should have been able to do something because he was a body-builder, He was not very tall but was described by members of staff as a 'mini-Arnold Schwarzenegger'! He said: 'I should have grabbed the gun and beaten him over the head with it and protected the women!'

I explained what I would like to do by 'reframing' his experience and he said that this was ok. I asked him to describe what had happened, how the man had come into the branch and how near to him he had put the shotgun. Peter was sitting down so I stood up, close to him, used two fingers representing the gun barrels and pointed them at him and asked him to move them to where the gun had been: the gun was about four inches from his eyes. I then asked him how the man was holding the gun and where his hands were. He described how the robber had his left hand on the stock of the gun so I asked him where his right hand and forefinger were and he said that the man's finger was on the trigger. I then asked him to pretend to grab the gun from me. There was a pregnant pause! He didn't try to grab the gun but looked at me and said, 'Bloody hell! He would have blown my head off'.

This dramatically changed his view of his reactions and of himself. He realised that had he pulled the gun forward, because the man's finger was on the trigger, the gun would almost certainly have fired. It might have missed him, it might not have been loaded, but he said that he was not prepared to take the chance and realised that if he had tried to grab the gun and failed, the robber could have shot either him or the female cashiers. His attitude towards himself and his involvement completely changed.

• Attempted rape

Jane, age 28, was walking along the path beside a river on the outskirts of a small town when a man approached her, asked for directions to the town centre, grabbed her, dragged her into some bushes and attempted to rape her. He placed a stiletto knife in her mouth, pricked the back of her throat and said that he would kill her if she didn't do what he wanted. However, after a few minutes he seemed to panic or realise what he was doing because he got up and ran away. Before Jane came to see me we had talked on the telephone where she described briefly what had happened and said that she understood about the debriefing process. She walked into the room, sat down and began to talk and as her story unfolded it was as if she was carrying on her back a huge ruck-sack full of the following:

'It was my fault'; 'Why had I stopped to talk to him?'; 'I should have been able to do something'; 'Why didn't I run away or scream?'; 'I should have fought back and kicked him'; 'I'm to blame for what happened'; 'I'm dirty and it's my fault'.

In saying what had happened she skipped very quickly over the part about the knife as though she had forgotten it or that it hadn't mattered, so, after listening for a while, I asked her to stop for a moment, go back to where the knife was produced and describe the knife and what he had done with it. She was reluctant to do it but, after a few deep breaths, began to talk about the knife and quite suddenly, and in mid-sentence, she stopped speaking. There was a long pause, she looked directly at me and said, clearly, and in a surprised voice, 'I now know why I feel like this. It's because of that bastard who tried to rape me!

It was as though a veil had been lifted from her: her body relaxed and she completely changed in the way she looked and in the way she was sitting and speaking. We then carried on with the rest of the story. After the debriefing, she said that she felt much better and more confident in herself, realised that it was not her fault and that she had been totally under his control: she could do nothing and realised that had she tried to resist she could have died. By helping her to explore the facts of what happened she was able to 'reframe' the incident. Two weeks later she rang me from abroad while on holiday with her boyfriend, thanking me for the debriefing and saying that she was coping very well.

- **The house fire**

The following story is based on a real incident and is slightly changed to avoid naming people or identifying the place where it happened. It demonstrates the way in which different people might react to and interpret the same event.

There was a fire in a house on the outskirts of a small town. On arrival, the fire and rescue crew were told by neighbours that there were three people trapped in the house so two officers put on their breathing apparatus and protective clothing, entered the building and, in one of the downstairs rooms, found three people unconscious, overcome by smoke and fumes. They were both able to carry someone from the house to safety but, as they left the building, the ceiling in the room collapsed and the third victim died. After the incident a local reporter spoke to one of the two officers and asked how it had been for him and how he felt about it. He was very positive and said:

> Well, we did our best. We saved two lives and if it hadn't been for us there would be three people dead. I am very sad about the third person but we did what we could, what was possible, and I think we did a really good job.

The reporter then asked the second officer the same questions and he said:

> I feel terrible. If only I had grabbed the other two people by the collar or clothes and dragged them out we could have saved all three. If only those idiots in the van hadn't pulled across the junction and stopped us at the traffic-lights, we could have been here a couple of minutes earlier. Why didn't the people in the houses opposite call us sooner? We could have rescued them all. It's our job to save lives. I feel awful. We failed.

The first officer saw the incident as an event where they had done their best under the circumstances and felt positive about it while still acknowledging the sadness of the death of the third person. The second officer saw it as an incident where they were useless and helpless and had failed and he felt guilty.

The first officer saw the cowboy on the horse but the second officer could only see a lot of black and white blotches which didn't make any sense and he reacted accordingly.

❖ Eye movement desensitising and reprocessing

In the USA, Dr Francine Shapiro was walking through a park one day and as she walked along, thinking, she realised that she was moving her eyes and began to notice that the movement of her eyes helped to reduce the symptoms of stress. Eventually, she devised the system known as 'Eye Movement Desensitising and Reprocessing', or EMDR, which is now widely used with people experiencing symptoms of stress and trauma or who develop PTS or PTSD. When conducting the session, the therapist sits in front of the client, fairly close, and asks the client to talk through and think about a disturbing incident in a traumatic event. While the client keeps his or her head perfectly still and talks, the therapist moves a finger slowly in front of the client's eyes from left to right, repeatedly, with the client's eyes following the finger.

The rationale for this might be partly based on REM or rapid eye movement, which can happen while we are asleep and, it is believed, signifies that we are dreaming and that the brain is processing emotional and other information. REM is thought by some to be the brain's way of sorting out events which happen in our lives so that we can cope with them. In post-traumatic stress and post-traumatic stress disorder, it seems that some memories are not processed and can become trapped within the nervous system and it is believed that eye movement during EMDR therapy helps the brain to process these memories. It is claimed by a colleague who is a qualified E.M.D.R. therapist that this procedure 'works like magic!'

• Moving eyes and tapping therapy

Some claim that the procedures used in EMDR might have links to similar techniques where, instead of the finger and eye movement, the therapist taps the left or right knee, wrists, head or arms or some other part of the person's body. Some therapists use a metronome as it clicks and swings from left to right. However, its origins might go even further back. In 1890, the

American psychologist and philosopher Dr William James, in his book The Principles of Psychology, suggested that when people's eyes move, they are thinking and that eye movements and how the brain interprets and processes information from experiences might be related. He thought that it is not just that the brain controls eye movement in the same way that the autonomic nervous system controls all our physical and internal bodily movements such as breathing, but that eye movement itself might influence how the brain works and processes information.

Figure 4
Eye Movements

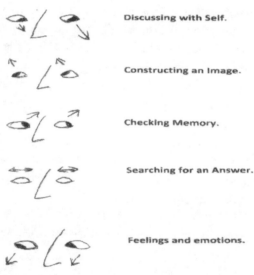

In the late 1980s, Dr Roger Callahan, an American psychologist who had studied traditional Chinese medicine, developed what he called 'Thought Field Therapy', sometimes known as 'Tapping Therapy'. The idea is that when we think of something, especially if it is disturbing or distressing, we are tuning in, like a radio or TV set, to our 'thought fields'. While the client concentrates on and repeats negative thoughts and emotions the therapist taps certain parts of the body called 'meridian points' and it is claimed that this can reduce tension and stress. Some claim that this therapy can reduce and alleviate stress in cases of phobias, panic attacks, depression, anger management, guilt and shame, obsessive compulsive disorder, various addictions such as smoking and obesity and in cases of PTSD.

In the early 1970s, Dr Richard Bandler and Dr John Grinder of the University of California conducted neurological research into eye movements and concluded that when eyes moved they are associated with activating certain parts of the brain. If you are talking and listening to someone, if you look at how and where their eyes are moving, by using what are called 'visual accessing clues' you can sometimes tell what they are thinking. In figure 4 , as you are looking at the eyes of another person, Looking down to the right on the diagram, means that the other person is looking down to their left and so on.

- Looking down to the right: they are conducting an internal dialogue and discussing something with the self.
- Looking down to the left: they are accessing emotions and feelings.
- Looking up to the right: they are checking memory and trying to remember a past experience, thinking logically and trying to construct a picture.
- Looking up to the left: they are visually constructing an image and relating it to the past and thinking about experiences and emotions.
- Eyes moving left to right: they are searching for an answer.

Generally, looking up, means that they are cognitively remembering and examining images and pictures of recent or past events and checking memory.

While looking down means that they are concentrating on emotions and feelings and conducting an internal enquiry.

All this suggests that eye movement might give clues to what someone is thinking or feeling and that using left to right eye movements, as in EMDR can, seemingly, influence the way the brain processes information.

❖ General treatment for PTSD

Treating PTSD is complex and usually involves therapy which can be in single sessions, one-to-one, with a psychiatrist, psychologist or counsellor, or in group therapy. Many techniques are used in treatment and one method is sometimes used in conjunction with other methods, for example:

- Psychotherapy, counselling and cognitive behavioural therapy (CBT).
- Eye movement desensitising and reprocessing (EMDR).
- Various forms of individual and group counselling or therapy.
- Defusing and psychological debriefing.
- Imaging techniques and guided fantasy.
- Medication and drugs.
- Relaxation techniques, including the use of audio CDs and tapes.
- Art therapy, painting, drawing and constructing collages.
- Catharsis – encouraging the release of emotions, thoughts, memories, feelings and physical sensations.
- Exercise and physical activities: walking, jogging, running, swimming.
- Recording or writing personal stories and listening to and/or reading them.

- Visiting the scene of the incident. This might be exposure therapy and part of the counselling process – see below.
- Exposure therapy, systematic desensitisation and flooding.
- Hobbies and interests: any hobbies, bee-keeping, gardening, listening to music and caring for animals such as horses.
- Hypnotherapy.
- Cultural and religious resources, reunions and memorial services.
- Education and giving information about reactions and teaching new coping strategies.
- Encouraging and facilitating family and social support.
- Alternative therapies: yoga, aromatherapy, reflexology, acupuncture, reiki and homoeopathy.

• **Exposure therapy** uses techniques such as asking someone to imagine the person, place, thing or situation which caused the trauma or anxiety, with the intention of desensitising the reaction to the image. Imaging and Guided Fantasy can be used to create relaxation by visualising safe, secure and peaceful situations such as sitting or lying in a meadow with the sun shining down, creating a feeling of peace and comfort.

• **Catharsis** encourages the release of emotions, sometimes hidden, such as fears and anxieties, usually through talking therapy.

• **Relaxation** techniques can be learned through listening to the voice of a counsellor or therapist, sometimes with soothing music playing in the background using earphones and special CDs or tapes with a personal player. This entails relaxing your body, beginning with tensing your toes and then relaxing them, gradually moving up your body, tensing and relaxing each part, until you reach your face muscles and head. This can help to relax your whole body's muscular system as well as your mind. Your GP or chemist can suggest where you can obtain relaxation CDs or tapes. Combat Stress, the Ex-Services' Mental Welfare Society, a civilian charity based in Leatherhead in Surrey, as well as a short course using individual and group therapy, now has a long in-house residential course to help ex-service personnel suffering from PTSD. Group therapy, sometimes based on cognitive behavioural therapy, uses cognitive techniques such as reframing and is usually used in a number of weekly sessions.

❖ Beware!

There are some therapists, counsellors, and other professionals offering help who have little or no training in or experience of treating traumatic stress. One local authority organisation offering group therapy based on CBT is not, I believe, cognitive, behavioural or therapy.

In one session on the course, the group leader, as part of what was supposed to be CBT, asked what the group would do if they were relaxing one sunny day in the garden and their neighbour was playing very loud music. When members of the group replied that they would go to his house and politely ask him to turn the volume down, he immediately said that this was not the right behaviour because it was 'being judgemental'. I dare not repeat the verbal and angry responses he received from the group! Weekly sessions were chaotic and ill-prepared and, on some occasions, the presenters could neither remember what they had done the previous week nor who had done it! On their final group session, because many members had left, other members of another group were brought in to take part. Promises of materials such as relaxation tapes and hand-outs were never kept and flip-chart presentations were written at an acute angle in tiny letters and were unreadable. At a conference I met a senior counsellor from a large counselling organisation who told me that she had worked with traumatised people and had conducted over a hundred debriefings. When I asked her where she was trained, the person she claimed had trained her in debriefing was known as someone who did not believe in it and she had trained on the telephone!

The following story is also an example of bad therapy.

James was working in a secure environment unit when an inmate, whom he knew well, committed suicide in front of him by cutting his throat. James was horrified and asked the organisation if he could see a counsellor and this was arranged. James walked into a room where the counsellor was sitting behind a desk and James was asked to sit in front of the desk. He explained very briefly to the counsellor what had happened. The counsellor then said to him, slowly and in a very quiet and patronising voice which rose up and down, 'James, tell me about your childhood'. James was surprised and angry and said so, but the counsellor replied that he needed to know what traumas James had experienced as a child. James said something I can't repeat but it rhymed with 'Look you!' and walked out disgusted and angry.

It is obvious that the counsellor didn't know how to counsel someone suffering traumatic reactions: where and how was he trained? He knew nothing about helping traumatised people or even where to sit during a session, certainly not hidden behind a desk and, what about the patronising voice?" Beware of helpers who can't help.

❖ Integration

I believe that the clue to treatment is that, as far as possible, those who suffer are helped to integrate their traumatic experiences into their lives.

'Don't try to leave the trauma behind'.

Sufferers can be likened to people walking along 'the road of life' trying to leave their painful and difficult reactions and experiences at the roadside. Imagine that, as you are walking along, your difficult and painful experiences are tied to you by an elastic rope, but you off-load them and leave them behind. As you walk away the elastic stretches until it reaches the point where it suddenly contracts and your past experiences hurtle into the present and hit you on the back of the head! Similarly, consciously or unconsciously, some people will bury reactions deep within their minds and might not wish to talk about them. If this is their way of coping, it should be respected, but for many people it is healthier to grasp these experiences, to face up to them, no matter how painful, and to incorporate and integrate them into their lives so that the experiences become part of who and what we are as persons.

We can tell our stories, express our feelings and try to forget them, but these reactions do not disappear, because our brains store the information about what we have experienced and how we have reacted. Many years after a traumatic event, we can usually remember what happened and some of the emotions and reactions we experienced at the time can return. If the incident has been integrated, we can still remember and feel these emotions, but they will not destroy our lives because we now view these memories and reactions as being part of our 'life-story' and we can cope with them. Some of the models and methods outlined in previous chapters might help us to move on to integration: looking at the coping strategies we use; life beliefs' theory and how we see ourselves and the world around us; the iceberg theory and whether or not we bury reactions; transactional analysis and what behaviours we have learned from our upbringing; cognitive reframing and

TRAUMA & TREATMENT   153

how we view and interpret the event. Also, are you an 'Independent' or a 'Klingon?' These might help you to understand why and how you have reacted to a traumatic experience and give some clues as to what can help.

Donald Meichenbaum, a Canadian psychologist, said that people with PTSD should be helped to feel that they have some element of control over their feelings and emotions and, by using cognitive restructuring, make sense of their senseless experiences. Therapy should engender feelings of personal growth and positive learning about oneself and the world and this can be achieved by the therapist establishing a positive relationship of trust with the client in a safe and comfortable environment where they are able to talk about what they have experienced. The aims are to give reassurance about the normality of reactions, to give help to recognise them and understand how and why reactions occur, and to give some hope for the future. Meichenbaum's major aim is 'integration' of the experience so that we can say: 'Even though there are still painful memories, they are now part of me and I can now live and cope with them."

Closure

Sometimes we hear the term closure used: 'I need to get closure!' If using the word 'closure' means that the incident is now over and gone, generally, I would question whether or not this experience has resulted in successful coping. However, if it means that someone is saying 'this traumatic experience has become part of me and my life as a person and, although there are still painful memories and emotions, I am learning to cope with it'. I would accept it. However, in some cases, coping can take a life-time. In experiences of loss, bereavement and grief, as with trauma, most people never get 'closure' in the sense that it is now over and gone. As previously said, most people will say: "you don't 'get over it, you go through it' and that they have learned, or are still learning, to cope, but that the experiences of loss, grief or trauma are not forgotten: "they never go away!"

A clergyman who lost a child in the Aberfan disaster recalled that it was common to visit someone who had also suffered the loss of a child and find that the experience, the pain and grief were still there. He said he asked one family, who were still grieving, how long ago their child, age four, had died and the reply was, 'forty years!' They would remember their child forever. What people might be saying when say they want closure is something I suggested earlier: 'In order to move on in my life I need to know what happened, if possible, to understand how and why it happened, how it has affected me and how I can cope with it'. But this can be a problem when there is no physical body to grieve over.

In 1988, a father and mother told me that they would never really move on until they saw their son's body. He was a soldier and had been killed in an explosion in Northern Ireland. Because of the injuries, they were advised not to see him, so all they saw was the sealed coffin at the funeral. They kept his returned belongings in their attic and every time I visited them, even many years later, the same scenario was re-enacted. They would tell me about his personal effects unopened in the attic and I would ask them the same question every time: why did they keep them? With a wry smile, they would always give the same answer: 'Just in case he needs them when he comes home!' Every Friday evening they still waited for his usual telephone call and, although they knew that he was dead, they still expected the telephone to ring. They are probably still waiting; this is not unusual or abnormal behaviour.

Not seeing his body had prolonged the intensity and extent of their grief and they will probably remember their child, and the dreadful pain his death has caused, until the day they die.

❖ How does your brain work?

One important development in looking at PTS and PTSD and in determining what treatment to offer is the research in trying to understand how our brains work and what processes take place in the brain when someone has a traumatic experience and develops traumatic reactions. Knowing how the brain operates might help us to understand why reactions develop and what treatments to offer those who suffer.

The limbic system

Research into the limbic system of the brain, which includes the amygdala, hippocampus and hypothalamus, suggests that when people are traumatised there are significant changes in the way the brain processes information coming in from the five senses. The limbic system is responsible for managing the autonomic nervous system, which regulates bodily functions: the involuntary movements and activities which we do not need to think about, such as breathing, digestion and our heart's beating.

• The amygdala

The amygdala is named after the Greek word for almond, and has been called the brain's early warning system. It is believed to be responsible for processing emotions such as fear, anger and pleasure and releases hormones such as cortisol and adrenalin into the body leading to the 'flight, fight or freeze' response. In traumatised people the amygdala can become active and hormones are released into the system even when there is no threat and people are frightened when there is nothing to be frightened about. This can happen when something such as a sight, touch, taste, sound or smell triggers a traumatic memory or it can come when there is no external stimulant. It is also thought that the amygdala is part of the system for processing information and determining what and where memories and stored.

• **The hippocampus**

The hippocampus helps to process and store information in the memory, particularly the laying down and processing of short-term memory into long-term memory, and, under certain circumstances, it can lose the ability to function correctly. Research in the USA suggests that prolonged stress can cause shrinkage of parts of the brain, especially the hippocampus. It is claimed that research with Vietnam veterans who developed PTSD showed a reduction in brain tissue in the hippocampus, which could result in cognitive impairment and memory loss.

• **The hypothalamus**

This exerts control of the sympathetic nervous system and controls hunger, thirst, body temperature, fatigue, glucose levels in the blood, sexual desire and mood and might be involved in regulating sleep. It can influence emotional responses and plays an important role in maintaining homeostasis: the cognitive-emotive balance in the brain.

Research is still in its infancy but could lead to greater understanding of how and why some people develop stress, traumatic reactions and PTSD, hopefully with positive results in terms of understanding the condition and in determining which treatment might be used.

Chapter 9

COPING WITH CRISIS

When someone retires from the armed services, they go on 'gardening leave': a period of four weeks during which they can do anything they wish as long as it relates to readjusting to civilian life.

❖ Social workers and stress

I retired from the army in 1992 and worked for the local county social services for a month, looking at the problem of stress and I spent the time interviewing social workers individually and confidentially. Most said that the major stresses did not come from their case-work but from the system and organisation, the bureaucracy and amount of paperwork involved, resulting in frustration, anger and feelings of isolation. Also, some managers were not in the same building as their teams and they therefore felt that they didn't care about them and were out of touch. One social worker said: 'If managers are not on the site, they will not be in sight and will not have insight!'

Another said, 'Those up there don't care about us down here!'

There were feelings of unreality and vulnerability, especially when dealing with difficult hostile or violent clients and there were occasions when workers were verbally and physically assaulted, sometimes resulting in symptoms of post-traumatic stress. Stresses did come from clients, but more from the volume and content of the work, the lack of resources and qualified staff and changes which were often implemented too quickly and without any preparation.

Workers often faced difficult and traumatic situations: child and partner abuse, long-term unemployment, marital problems, breakdown and separation, adoption, fostering, removal of children from a parent or parents, poverty, attempted suicide, people with mental and physical disabilities, single parents struggling to survive, murder, pregnancy, birth, old age and death. So, how did they cope? Coping strategies mentioned in Chapter 5 were used and 'distancing' was common.

- Distraction by thinking of something else.
- Numbing emotions when dealing with difficult cases.
- Being grateful for their own lives, especially partners and families.
- Lack of sympathy for those who moaned and complained about trivialities.
- Limiting exposure to clients
- Feelings of being a 'professional' and knowing what to do.
- Having a sense of purpose and listening and talking to colleagues.
- Being a member of a team and using mutual and group support.
- Using hobbies, exercise, sport and music.
- Concentrating on the job in hand.
- Not thinking of clients as 'real people'.
- Using sick humour, but not about children.
- Expressing emotions and feelings using 'good old Anglo-Saxon expletives'.
- Talking to the cat, dog, a photograph or some other object.

For many, another major factor causing stress was that their training, although extensive, had not prepared them to deal with their own inner and emotional reactions to their work. One very experienced woman commented:

> I was trained as a decision maker and problem solver and believed that it was my job to make people feel better. But there was little or no preparation for me to face the distress, anger, hurt, sadness, grief, rejection and frustration that I might feel.

There were cases of 'breakdown' and depression and some experienced acute and long-term stress and said they had developed symptoms typical of PTS and PTSD. Although they were supposed to have one-to-one supervision on a regular basis, many said that this hardly ever took place, but all agreed about the need for regular and personal supervision and support. A report, identifying high stress levels amongst personnel, resulted in the appointment of a stress and trauma counsellor.

❖ Consultancy – working with trauma

On retiring from the army in 1992, I set up a consultancy on counselling and trauma and began to work with aid agencies, counselling and debriefing people following traumatic events including some who had experienced long-term exposure to trauma, such as aid-workers returning from overseas.

• The Rwanda crisis – 1994

In the spring of 1994 a crisis arose in Rwanda, in Africa, where conflict arose between the two major groups, the Hutu and the Tutsi people. Simplifying the situation, the Tutsi were considered to be the better educated and the ruling class and this caused problems and tribal tension. This resulted in genocide, some saying that approximately one million people were massacred:

sometimes neighbour murdering neighbour!

A health unit from a major aid agency contacted me asking what they should do about the possibility of their workers developing psychological problems while overseas and of having difficulties on their return to the UK. Preparation for their personnel already included practical, political, social and cultural education but no information was given about stress reactions and the possibility of psychological or personal problems. One problem was that some aid workers had responded to an advertisement and, within a very short time, they were overseas in a dramatic, distressing and traumatic environment. Also, they could be employed on short-term contracts of six months or so and then return to a 'normal' life in the UK with no assessment or help. I suggested a number of strategies: the importance of educating all personnel, including managers, especially those going overseas, about any possible psychological, social, emotional and physical reactions they might experience; support for them while there and some form of assessment, debriefing and monitoring on their return. As standard procedure, there should be regular supervision and informal meetings for all personnel. Some managers could be trained in the technique of defusing with an individual or a group which might be as simple as just getting people together regularly to talk and share experiences.

Aid workers can encounter many different kinds of traumatic incidents: extreme poverty, injustice, war and conflict, overwhelming numbers of refugees, the injured, the sick and dying and people who have been bereaved, tortured, mutilated, raped, imprisoned, intimidated, beaten, kidnapped and held hostage. They can also experience personal problems. Situations were often chaotic, leading to questions about responsibility and not being clear about who was in charge or who should be helped, by whom, how and when; communication was sometimes poor so that they were not sure what was happening around them. Life could seem unpredictable, particularly because of the vast numbers of refugees and the confusing and sometimes dangerous environment. There could be fear of being injured or killed and, even with colleagues around them, feelings of isolation, loneliness and concerns about safety. There were also bizarre and horrific instances which caused 'cognitive dissonance': the internal confusion caused when facing, at the same time, two very different and conflicting experiences.

In Rwanda, some aid workers were living away from the refugee camps and staying in a hotel where, in the evenings during dinner, gentle and soothing music was playing in the background while dead bodies were floating past in the lake. Some were told to lock the doors of their vehicles when travelling and, should they hit, injure or even kill anyone, not to stop in case they were attacked. Also, they were directed not to give out food other than during an official distribution. This resulted in feelings of guilt, and anger and problems with driving after returning home because such behaviour is contrary to the way they would normally react or respond to those in need.

In some cases, when aid workers returned home, they met senior members of staff and were asked about practical and operational matters but were seldom asked how they were or about their experiences, how they had coped or how they were feeling and coping now. This could be left to health, welfare and medical staff, but other people showing an interest and that they care is important. Some had difficulty in adjusting and experienced manic behaviour, tension, hyper-vigilance and irritability. Also, working overseas could become addictive leading to feelings of guilt, especially for leaving local colleagues behind and believing that 'I should be out there, helping'. For some it also caused difficulties in relationships with a partner or family and in settling into 'normal' home life. Most aid workers said they could speak about their experiences but some did not wish to talk and it was a common experience for workers to say that when they did talk people could appear to be bored or uninterested and, in any case, they didn't understand. Having been in a situation of high drama resulted in some workers experiencing symptoms of post-traumatic stress and feeling that 'normal' life back home was mundane, shallow and even pointless. They had 'flashbacks' and disturbed sleep patterns, dreams and nightmares, were unable to rest or relax, had bouts of irritability, anger and withdrawal and physical or emotional isolation from family and social life.

Defusings or Debriefings were held with those returning home and, although these were not compulsory, most opted to take part and some even asked 'when am I having my debriefing?'

In these sessions, reactions were typical of stressed and traumatised groups and individuals. Some said that when they returned, they found it very difficult to adjust their lives to their 'normal' environment.

> How can you sit and watch television or walk into a supermarket when, a short time ago, you have seen, at first hand, hunger, poverty, disease, threat and death?

> How should you react to children playing or people laughing and to normal life in the UK, when you have seen children and people starving and dying?

'Cognitive dissonance' again! In many ways the psychological and emotional reactions of some aid workers mirror the reactions of armed services' personnel when returning home from conflict and war.

An aid worker who returned to the UK said that certain days were very difficult to face because they were the days when people put out their rubbish in the street in black plastic bags for collection. On these days he found it almost impossible to walk down the street and, when he did, he would begin to shake and had to look away and hold his breath because his abiding memory of these large, black, plastic bags was that they were used overseas for dead bodies! He said that black, plastic bags resulted in feelings of nausea, fear, anger, horror, helplessness and grief. One difficulty with counselling or debriefing aid-workers was that sometimes they experienced trauma over extended periods.

Ken was sent to an East-European country by an aid agency, was there for nine months, and on his return he asked for a debriefing. Although the debriefing was at his request, he started the session by saying that he wasn't clear why he had come because he had not experienced any difficult, disturbing or traumatic incidents. He talked about joining the organisation and going overseas so I asked him to say what his first impressions were on arrival and then to describe three occasions where he was anxious, felt helpless, worried, angry or frightened. He thought for a brief moment, talked about his first impressions, and then said that on one occasion, travelling in a car with others, they were terrified when stopped by armed men who took all their belongings and personal items and he thought that they were going to be shot. Next, he said he was in his office in a town, when the building was targeted by mortar and machine-gun fire and he had hidden under his desk in fear. Finally, he said he did have serious personal problems with his manager where he felt angry, isolated and ignored. I decided to conduct three mini-debriefings, using these three incidents in one long session, and afterwards he said that he had found this helpful and was glad that he had come.

When aid workers live in traumatic situations for long periods of time, the length of time overseas results in an increase in problems and reactions and some will come to the conclusion that the world is meaningless, random, unjust and malevolent and experience a deep sense of helplessness and low self-esteem. However, in spite of the problems, most aid workers coped very well and, even when they developed difficult reactions, most described their work as not only necessary but also 'fulfilling, useful and effective'.

❖ Ongoing situations of stress

Ongoing stress is not confined to aid workers. Other people, who might not even be noticed, can also experience psychological and emotional trauma over long periods of time, such as people living in abusive relationships or being bullied. A police officer might be involved for some weeks after an event, investigating the scene, visiting and helping bereaved individuals and families, writing reports and, perhaps, attending funerals of colleagues or victims. Telephonists or typists in the emergency services, media or other organisations, can be listening to or typing reports about ongoing traumatic incidents and are also at risk of developing symptoms of stress and trauma, as are reporters, photographers and camera operators. After the vicious and horrendous murder of a child by other children, someone holding the long extended microphone to pick up information from reporters, interviewees and police officers developed symptoms of post-traumatic stress. These people need to be remembered and, where necessary, monitored and helped, especially as reactions to traumatic experiences can emerge many months or even years later.

- ## The Aberfan disaster 1966

On 21 October 1966, a mountain of debris from the local coal tip surged down like the lava flow from a volcano or an avalanche and engulfed the local school and part of the village. One hundred and forty-four people were killed, including one hundred and sixteen children, five teachers and twenty-three other adults. This event continued for many days and the aftermath is still felt to this day by some of those who helped at the scene, the bereaved, and villagers, some of whom are still receiving counselling or therapy. Delayed reactions are common.

In 1994 I was taking a seminar on bereavement and loss at Bristol University and, as part of the session, said I was going to show a short video about Aberfan. There were no comments from the group so, at the appropriate moment, I played the video. About five seconds after it started a man screamed, jumped to his feet and ran out of the room, followed by a friend. At the end of the session I found him standing in the corridor, shaking and sweating. He apologised for what had happened and said that at seventeen he had been an apprentice miner in the next valley to Aberfan and immediately went with a rescue team to help at the scene and the short video clip had resurrected hidden and horrific memories and experiences. He said it had been a most terrible and distressing time but he joined the army and thought that the incident had gone away. He added that he was surprised that the reactions and memories were still there after twenty-eight years!

- ## The Hillsborough disaster 1989

On 15 April 1989, in the stadium of Sheffield Wednesday football team, 94 people were crushed to death. Over seven hundred people were injured, many of whom were Liverpool supporters under the age of thirty.

One young man died after four days and the death toll reached 96, four years later, when a man on a life-support system died in hospital.

In 1999 I was running a course at Bristol University about coping with trauma. As I did with the Aberfan video, I told the course that I was going to use a video about Hillsborough to show the reactions of some helpers from the emergency services. Immediately, a man, who was a trained therapist, stood up and quietly said he would have to leave the room. I started the video and left the room to see if I could find him. He was outside, walking up and down in the corridor, visibly shaken. He was stunned and embarrassed but apologised and said that he couldn't watch anything about Hillsborough because he had a ticket for the game but, for some reason, he couldn't go. He had self-diagnosed this as 'survivor guilt' and was having counselling help. This was ten years after the event and, because of survivor guilt, viewing a video of the disaster was more than he could bear. Remember the iceberg theory and how past experiences although deeply hidden, can emerge with devastating effect?

• Nairobi 1998 – the bombing of the US embassy
On 7 August 1998, the US Embassy in Nairobi was attacked by terrorist bombers and most of the building destroyed. Estimates of casualty figures vary but some two hundred and fourteen people were killed and about four thousand injured. Two days later I was contacted by the Foreign and Commonwealth Office in London and asked if I would go to Kenya because members of the British High Commission in Nairobi had heard the explosions and had gone to the embassy almost immediately to help. They knew their counterparts in the embassy, some of whom were close friends and colleagues who often worked and socialised together. Also, some members of staff were medically qualified

and had set up a triage station in the US Embassy car park. There were also local drivers of cars and other members of staff who had helped at the scene. All involved from the High Commission had done a superb job in what they had been able to do and in the ways they had responded to what was, for them, an incident which had caused the deaths of many people known to them.

I was to go to Nairobi with a senior member of their health department and their senior counsellor, and we decided to have a meeting to discuss what we would do. We agreed that, with the co-operation and permission of staff, we would offer information, hopefully to normalise reactions, informal debriefing and personal counselling as necessary but would be ready to adapt our plans to respond to whatever people said they wanted. Also, we would meet with managers, supervisors and team-leaders to discuss what had happened and to talk about the purpose of the visit. We wanted to visit the scene of the bombing and the surrounding area and find out what people's expectations and needs were: what had been done to help them, who had been involved, which groups or teams, how and where they were involved and why and in what ways people had reacted during and following the incident. We also wished to discuss our plans and possible strategies such as the use of debriefing and counselling and to explain what these involved. Finally, we wanted to look at post-visit procedures for support, monitoring of personnel and to discuss what resources or help might be needed.

When we arrived in Nairobi it was clear that members of staff were much comforted simply by the fact that the Foreign and Commonwealth Office had sent us to help. When we met senior members of staff at the airport, and when we walked around the Commission to meet people, we were greeted like long lost friends. Also, members of staff had heard of the support measures used in other missions in Nairobi in the American, Dutch, Canadian and Australian missions, where a form of debriefing was being used, and they were keen to have similar procedures.

On the first morning we met senior members of staff and in the afternoon met all those involved to say why we were there and what we had to offer. The Debriefing process was explained and they agreed to attend and take part although it was explained to them that they need not answer any questions or speak if they did not wish to do so. We decided to have two Debriefing groups and we asked them how they wanted to be split up because there were those who had worked in the site and those like drivers who had helped on the periphery doing important jobs such as delivering and distributing food and drinks. Some of these drivers, and other members of staff, though not directly involved at the site, were as much at risk of psychological disturbance as anyone else because they had to stand and wait outside the Embassy and could see what was happening. When we mentioned splitting them into two groups, like the wives held hostage in Iraq, staff members decided to split themselves up into two groups without reference to seniority or position. The debriefings seemed to go well and because one local driver present only spoke Swahili, we worked with him through a translator.

For the next three days we ran the debriefing sessions, had a number of other meetings, talked to staff from the British Council in Nairobi, ran a listening skills course at the request of staff and gave one-to-one counselling sessions for those who said that they needed to talk further. The listening skills course was requested because some members of staff wished to be sure that they were listening to and picking up what other people were, or were not saying and wished to be able to respond in an empathic and appropriate manner. They also wanted to be able to monitor and assess responses and reactions to the incident, including their own, and to see if there might be a need for referral. There were also a number of lunches, dinners and drinks' parties and these were important because they gave us an opportunity to meet informally and talk with partners and wives. We spent one morning and evening seeing individuals who had requested one-to-one counselling during which we were presented with reactions and concerns resulting from the bombing, but some also wished to talk about personal matters and family problems. Because of the situation and confidentiality, it would not be right to mention specific reactions or problems but typical reactions to a traumatic event were present.

On the fourth day we were taken to visit a baby elephant sanctuary and the Nairobi Game Park where we saw lots of giraffes and antelope, but no lions! Before we returned to the UK, we met together, to support each other and to discuss what had happened and how we were feeling. We bade farewell and flew back home.

- Suicide 1996

I was asked by a senior social worker to conduct a debriefing with her and 24 of her colleagues because a member of the team had committed suicide. After the usual self-introductions and explanation of the rules and procedure of debriefing, I began by asking Ann (not her real name), the first woman on my right in the circle, to say when and how she had first met and come to know Mary. She immediately became angry and said that this was irrelevant as she wanted to talk about her friend, about what had happened and about her own sense of loss. I gently but firmly said that in the introduction she had agreed with everyone else to abide by the rules, so I asked her to hold on to her strong feelings and emotions and that if she felt she could not answer the question I would go around the group and she could then answer if and when she felt comfortable about it. The question was simply asking about her first encounter with Mary. Ann wanted immediately to tell me what her emotional reactions were to her friend's suicide but had I allowed her to do this it could have triggered others into an emotional free-for-all and destroyed the session. Ann composed herself and then told me how and when she had first met Mary and what her impressions were at that time. After this initial hiccup the debriefing went smoothly as each individual story enfolded. There were the usual initial reactions of shock, disbelief, sadness and anger. Some said that perhaps they had not been friendly enough or accepting of Mary and others said that they had been unable to relate to her and didn't really know her very well and felt guilty because of this. Some expressed reactions of surprise that Mary should have killed herself but everyone spoke about the enormous pressures they were all under at work and the despair, depression and disillusionment Mary might have felt. There were also comments from a few saying that they didn't know anything about Mary's personal and private life and wondered if this had anything to do with what she had done. All who knew her as a friend said that they were totally unaware of any indications beforehand of what she would do and this seemed to help those who said they felt guilty because they didn't know her well. Most said that they should have recognised the signs, but all agreed that there weren't any. At the end of the debriefing, everyone said that they accepted and understood the different ways in which they and others had reacted and that hearing others say how they had reacted and felt had been helpful and reassuring. Including two short breaks and a break for lunch, the Debriefing took just under six hours.

• Working with organisations

As well as working with a number of aid agencies, I worked for five years for a large building society, conducting their post-armed robbery debriefings and counselling. I also started running courses for many organisations, including the three emergency services, social services and educational psychology and disaster management departments in a number of counties. The aims were clear: to challenge and change unhelpful attitudes towards traumatic reactions by educating personnel about the effects of stress and trauma on individuals and the possibility of the development of PTS and PTSD, and to emphasise the need for appropriate resources for referral. One major problem with organisations was that, although there was enthusiasm from some people, there were occasions when there was little or no support from higher management. As one course member said, in some cases it seemed that managers were 'just keen to tick the boxes'.

Although our knowledge, understanding and treatment of PTS and PTSD has grown and developed over the years there are still some people who have their own unmoveable beliefs and deny that psychological symptoms are real. Many sufferers have said, 'If I had a broken arm or leg, people would understand but some people think I am shirking'. These people are the 'unbelievers', who still exist in every part of society, both civilian and military.

❖ The Unbelievers

PTSD is now generally accepted as a genuine psychiatric condition and not the result of personal weakness or inadequacy, but there are still sceptics who blame the individual and tend to see the desire for compensation as the driving force behind those who campaign or work in the area of trauma. We are still left with the

problems of stigma, lack of understanding and of un-
§helpful attitudes, perhaps from some amongst our
own families, friends or colleagues, towards those who
develop psychological problems. Although many new
initiatives have been taken by governments, there is
still a shortage of appropriate resources and funding
for treatment throughout the UK, especially for those
leaving the armed services. Whether a civilian or
military sufferer, there are still some who believe that
your reactions are not natural or normal and that there
is something wrong with you as an individual.

A senior ex-army officer, now a senior administrator
at a university, who I met frequently, when I was to lead
a seminar on stress, trauma and PTSD, always took the
opportunity to confront me beforehand over a cup of
coffee and tell me, with a firm but detached smile, that
he had seen many horrible things during his time in the
army, including experiences of combat, but that in all his
military service he had never been affected in any way
and had never suffered psychologically or experienced
any stress reactions or disturbing symptoms. He seemed
to view this as a personal challenge to me and to the
whole subject of stress and trauma. But, was he telling
the truth? The coffee was always very good!

It is interesting when people say this kind of thing
and I wonder what's going on inside them and why they
feel the need to say it, especially those who repeat it
over and over again. I am reminded of the following
words: 'Whenever we deny our own pain, our ability to
perceive the pain in others diminishes.'

There are some who do not react overtly in a physical
or psychological way to traumatic events and do cope
well and it might be the case that the experience has not
affected them at all and that it will simply be something
they remember from their past as disturbing, or not
disturbing in any way. It is possible that this officer is

simply telling the truth and has never suffered from
any kind of traumatic stress, but it is the fact that he
has to challenge me and tell me the same story each
time that makes me wonder. Is he just stating a fact
or is he defending and protecting his own hidden
pain? If this is the case, he might not even be aware
of some experiences or emotions buried deep in his
unconscious.

Of those involved in traumatic events, whether in war
or in civilian incidents, most will cope well, but some will
be disturbed either at the time or afterwards and some
will not experience or show symptoms of stress until
many months or even many years later. Because some
do cope well does not mean that those who react in a
different way are lesser persons. Reactions are not signs
of a lack of moral fibre or of some form of personality
disorder. Sometimes those within organisations who
wish to understand stress and trauma are not helped by
attitudes from above.

I was running a two-day course for police officers in
understanding stress, trauma, PTS and PTSD. A woman
inspector came to see me at the first morning coffee
break and asked if she could speak to me on my own.
She said that she was angry with her chief inspector and
that I should know what her situation was at work. She
was keen to learn about stress and trauma but, when
she applied to go on the course, her senior officer
called her into his office and asked what the course
was about. When she told him the purpose and of her
interest in trauma he described it as a 'tree-hugging'
course and said quite firmly, 'You can go, but don't bring
any of your f*****g problems to me!' Not very helpful,
understanding or caring, but not an unusual response!

One interesting point about running such courses
for the emergency services and other organisations
is that when I have been asked to run a course on

understanding stress, trauma and PTSD, more often than not it was at the instigation of someone at a very low level of command. In one case it was a police constable who had badgered his seniors in the county until they agreed to do something about it and to have some education and training for officers. Rarely has the request been from someone high up in the line of responsibility.

The only occasion I have been involved in running courses where the initial interest has come directly from 'the top' was with a county fire and rescue service where the 'fire chief' had requested it. He had attended a course with other senior officers at the Emergency Planning College at Hawkhills near Easingwold in North Yorkshire, where the subject was raised. He returned to his command and declared that every officer, of station officer and above would attend a course educating them about the subject. The majority of officers on the courses welcomed the opportunity to look at the subject of trauma, post-traumatic stress and PTSD, but there were still the unbelievers! However, sometimes an unbeliever can make the real point and purpose of a course.

On one of these courses, Leslie, a fire and rescue officer, was very uncomfortable and cynical about the topic of trauma and PTSD. At the beginning of the course, when course members were introducing themselves, he added that he thought that the subject was a waste of time, that there were no such things as stress and traumatic reactions and he gave the age old mantra familiar to me from army life and elsewhere: 'If you can't take a joke, you shouldn't have joined and if you can't stand the heat, get out of the kitchen!'

There was a long pause, he looked around at his colleagues, looked very uncomfortable and said: 'Mind you, I am going through a very difficult time at present and finding it very hard and upsetting because my wife is leaving me and taking the children with her'.

Before I could say anything, another officer said very quietly: 'Well, Leslie, you know what they say? 'If you can't take a joke, you shouldn't have joined!'

There was general laughter and Leslie looked a bit sheepish, but when the laughter had died down he said: 'Thanks mate! Point taken!'

Needless to say, he was a very valuable contributor to the rest of the course.

During the Rwanda crisis I was debriefing many people returning from Africa and one day was in Oxford shopping with my wife. We went to have coffee in the centre of the covered market and the following took place.

My wife sat down and I saw two rather well dressed ladies sitting at the next table. In the army we would have referred to them as part of 'the twin-set and pearls brigade'. I went for the coffee, returned to our table and noticed that the two ladies had gone. My wife said, 'It's a good job you weren't here a few minutes ago!' When I asked why, she said that the two women were talking about Oxfam, Rwanda and aid workers and one had said very loudly to the other, 'Yes, my dear. Aren't those Oxfam people wonderful? They go overseas and see the most horrible things and, do you know, it doesn't affect them one little bit!' Little did she know!

In 1994 I was running a course in London entitled 'Understanding and Coping with PTS and PTSD'. During the morning coffee break I was standing with a small group of women when a very large man, about six feet four inches tall and with a huge paunch, eased his way into the group. He immediately said that he was enjoying the course so far but didn't agree with all this talk about stress and trauma. He was a retired police sergeant who had served for over thirty years and said that he had never suffered from any stress reactions. 'You name it, I've seen it all: dead or burnt people, dead babies and children, people swinging from the rafters, squashed bodies in road traffic accidents and the rest and it has never affected me one little bit!' There was a pregnant pause! One of the women in the group said quietly, 'So you were in lots of traumatic situations then? What did you do after any of these?' He looked around the group and said very hesitantly, 'Well ... it wasn't so bad. Mind you, I often couldn't sleep at night and would lie awake until three or four o'clock in the morning'. 'So, what did you do when you couldn't sleep?' asked the woman. There was another pause, and he said, with a combined element of strained bravado and embarrassment, 'Well, in the middle of the night, when I couldn't sleep, I would talk to my wife for hours'. The group stirred and the woman said, 'And who did your wife talk to? There was a chuckle in the group and he began to laugh. I think that the point had been made!

One quite extraordinary reaction came from a group of fire and rescue officers attending a similar course.

During the coffee break I was standing with five experienced officers, all from the same county, who knew each other well and had worked together for many years. Brian, one of the officers, said, 'We all know about PTSD don't we lads? George, here', and he pointed to one member of the group, 'has had PTSD, haven't you George?' George nodded as did everyone. 'Yes!' Brian said, 'You were off work for over six months weren't you George, having treatment? But you're all right now aren't you?' All in the group nodded sympathetically, including George. There was a long pause and Brian looked around the group, gave a short, self-conscious laugh, and said, 'But we all know that there's no such thing as PTSD, don't we?' This was greeted with more nodding heads. Poor old George didn't say a word, but he didn't nod his head! Some defence mechanisms are extremely strong and persistent.

❖ You are normal!

One message of this book, central to our understanding of stress and trauma, has been emphasised a number of times: no matter how you react to stressful and traumatic events, your reactions are natural and normal for you so don't compare yourself with anyone else. The reactions are yours but what initially triggered them is usually an incident over which you had little or no control. It sounds too simple, but, 'If the incident had not happened, you would not have reacted as you did. It wasn't your fault so don't blame yourself'. Also, it is normal to react to traumatic events in different ways at different times because even similar incidents are not identical and your reactions depend on a number of factors: how traumatic the event was and how long it lasted; your emotional and physical state at the time; how prepared you were for what happened; how you were treated and supported during and after the event and how you interpreted it. Sometimes just knowing you are 'normal' can help.

After I retired from the army, my first book, *Post-Trauma Stress*, was published in 1993. Shortly afterwards the telephone rang one Sunday evening when I was away from home. My wife answered the call and a woman asked if this was the home of Frank Parkinson and could she please speak to him. My wife said that I was out but that she could take a message or, if she gave her telephone number, I would call her back when I returned. There was a pause and then the woman said, 'I have been reading his book. Just tell him "thank you" for page eighty-seven'. My wife said that she didn't understand. The woman replied, 'My son died two years ago and I thought I was going mad until I read page eighty-seven!' A great sense of relief can register on someone's face when they realise that, 'What I am feeling and experiencing is normal and natural'. However, reactions of stress and traumatic stress can result in PTS or PTSD.

❖ Recovering

When working or living with traumatised people or when you are suffering, remember:

- Given time, most people will cope and recover and, depending on the nature of the incident, most reactions usually begin to diminish within a month or so. Note: this does not apply to bereavement and grief or to PTSD.
- Some will need specialist help from medical, psychological, psychiatric or counselling services: usually referred by a GP.
- A few will suffer from PTSD and develop personal, social, family, health and psychological problems, either at the time or later, even months or years later.
- Symptoms might emerge immediately after an incident but can lie dormant for many months and, in some cases, for years.
- Different treatments help different people: there is no panacea for all ills.
- Most people will always remember and recall a traumatic event or experience but, hopefully, it will eventually be integrated into and become part of their lives.

❖ Military reservists and civilians at risk

One group of special concern are those military and civilian personnel who have served in places such as Iraq and Afghanistan but are not 'regulars' but were in the Territorial Army (now known as the Army Reserve), reserve units of the Royal Navy and Royal Air Force or have worked for civilian organisations. Some part-timers or civilians who have served in a combat zone have returned home to their lives where they do not have the presence and support of colleagues and comrades and the camaraderie of the military culture, environment and way of life. Some of these people will go home to their families and civilian jobs and suffer in silence. Unfortunately, some civilian health and welfare agencies do not have the experience, knowledge, resources or training to recognise the problem and do not have facilities to support and help those who suffer. A number of charities are involved in helping sufferers, ex-service personnel and their families and civilians, but, unless they are referred by a GP, the onus is on the individual to contact them. However, as was said earlier, the symptoms of stress, PTS and PTSD, including shame, the fear of stigma and the natural defence of denial, can mean that some do not self-refer. This also applies to civilians suffering from events other than war or combat: living with an abusive partner or being bullied at work; a 'carer' with little or no support; involvement in a serious traffic accident; being kidnapped, held hostage or mugged; being raped or sexually abused. These people can be increasingly at risk of developing stress or traumatic reactions and will need help.

Once service personnel develop psychological problems many are quickly discharged from a military environment and depend on the civilian medical services in the NHS, where the availability, quality and nature of care and resources for helping can vary. In recent years, research in the UK suggests that the vast majority of ex-service personnel prefer to be treated by military staff in a military environment and this can be a problem for those who suffer and can prevent them from looking for or accepting help.

In the civilian world all GPs should have the skills to identify the possibility that a patient might be suffering from PTS or PTSD and be able to refer them to the appropriate professionals for help.

Psychological problems, whether with civilians, members of the emergency services or military personnel can still be viewed with cynicism and suspicion and those who suffer can feel misunderstood, neglected and rejected by society at large. What they seek is the dignity of recognition of their plight and appropriate treatment and help.

❖ The war against trauma goes on!

One of my retired pleasures is that I am on the 'Speakers' List' for the Women's Institute for the counties of Wiltshire and Oxfordshire where I talk about the need to understand PTS and PTSD. On a number of occasions, after the talk and questions, an elderly lady has come up to me, asks to speak to me privately and says quietly: 'Thank you for the talk. I now know what has been wrong with my husband since he came home from the Second World War!'

This also applies to other conflicts. Another woman said that she now knew why her husband behaved in the way he did: he had been in a serious traffic accident some years ago where he was badly injured and shocked but had never talked about it.

There is help available and I hope that this book has given some clues not only about how people suffer but also some ideas about why, and what can be done to help. If you are suffering, I hope that this book has given you the knowledge and strength to seek help and to move on in your life.

In 1995, after I left the army, I was invited to present a paper on psychological debriefing at an international conference in Kuwait where I met two American psychologists. Something they said in their presentation about treatment and helping people who have experienced a traumatic event and are suffering, summarises much of the experiences, ideas and information given in this book.

The disorders of extreme stress, recalled in survivors of war, atrocities, combat, violence, terrorism and torture, require that therapists listen to their clients' stories with patience, respect, credibility and compassion; that they provide a safe and secure place to revisit their traumas; that they help them reframe the expectations and attributions which were shaped in the traumatic experience; that they guide them towards coping skills which help their clients to integrate and adapt their experiences into the present.

Appendix A

COPING WITH STRESS AND TRAUMA

❖ Coping with stress

If you are experiencing stress at home, work or elsewhere, some of these methods might reduce the reactions.

• Physical and Emotional Reactions

When you are stressed, certain changes 'automatically' take place in your body: you have little or no control over them. The release of certain hormones, such as adrenaline and cortisol, into your system result in changes: your mouth goes dry, your muscles become tense and ready to react, your vision becomes focused and the adrenaline gives you the energy either to fight the threat or to run away. Alternatively, you might freeze and react with denial, disbelief and bewilderment and, temporarily, you can lose the power of thought and speech. You might also be unable to make decisions and experience feelings of irritability, anger, an exaggerated startle response and 'jumpiness', physical tightness in the chest and an increase in both heart rate and breathing. However, you might react, as did Charles Dickens after the train crash, by calmly helping those who are injured or distressed, or you might just stand there, dazed and bewildered, wondering what has happened.

The following are suggested strategies for coping by

identifying the source of the stress and looking at ways which might help you to cope with the symptoms. It can help if you write down your reactions or answers to some of the comments and questions.

❖ Coping with stress – strategies

- **Identify the source of the stress**

Try to identify your main emotions or feelings. What feelings were aroused in you when you began to feel stressed? Is it a combination of reactions? Attempt to discover where these emotions came from, what caused them and try to link them to the source of the emotions and reactions. Ask yourself the following questions and try to give more than a one word, or a 'yes' or 'no', answer.

Is the stress from something external?

- Who or what caused the stress?
- Is it from a particular situation or incident?
- Is it from an individual or an organisation or group of people?

Is the stress from something internal?

- Is it something about you, your attitude, belief or the way you are thinking and can you change or adjust any of these?
- Is it due to a present experience or is it connected with something from the past?
- What do you feel inside: anger, fear or some other emotions?

- **Be positive**

No matter how difficult or painful, accept your emotions and feelings as being normal and natural for you and the result of what you have experienced or are experiencing.

- Try to direct the reactions to where or with whom they belong.
- Find a suitable and appropriate way to express your emotions. If it helps, shout, swear or express your feelings in a way you find natural. You might prefer to do this when you are alone rather than in public.
- What can you do to change your situation or position?
- Can you talk positively and realistically to anyone concerned or involved: can you find someone you trust and talk to confidentially?
- Do not necessarily think that the stress is your fault and that you are to blame: as before, ask yourself who or what is the cause?
- Be assertive rather than aggressive

Do you believe the following about being assertive?
- You have a right to be angry sometimes and express how you feel.
- You have a right to be wrong, sometimes.
- You are not perfect and neither are other people.
- You have a right to put your own needs first, sometimes.
- You have a right to be listened to, respected and acknowledged.
- You have a right to say 'no!' without giving an explanation.

Do you believe that these statements are your rights as a human being? You sometimes need to assert these rights, especially in situations where others assume that you do not have them. For example, how often do people make unreasonable demands on you where you feel obliged to do what they want you to do? You don't want to do it, but you do it and then complain about it afterwards. You want to say 'no' but say 'yes' and then feel angry and inconvenienced and your stress levels rise. You ask: 'Why didn't I say no in the first place?'

If you say 'no', do you think you have to give an explanation but then feel guilty about saying 'no'? I learned from my father-in-law to say 'no!' One day I asked him if he would like to come with me and my wife into town where he could look in the bookshops and we would treat him to lunch. He replied, 'Well, thank you very much for thinking about me and being so kind. Thank you, but no!' No explanation given!

• **Previous coping**

Is this something you have experienced before or is it a new experience? If you have previously felt like this, what have you learned about how you coped at the time and what was the result?

• **Rehearse and be prepared**

If you need to speak to someone on the telephone or meet them, go through in your mind what you are going to say. It can help if you write it down and rehearse it in front of a mirror. Stick to your agenda, don't be put off, and ensure that you 'have your say'. However, you might rehearse it but, when you are in the situation, 'nerves' take over and you might fail. Take a number of deep breaths before you begin, try to control your breathing and remember your rights.

• **Be realistic**

Are any of your expectations unrealistic, either about yourself or of others? Are you attempting the impossible and are you aiming too high – or too low? Try to be certain of the 'facts' about what has caused the reactions and problems.

• **Acceptance or change**

What would be the consequences of accepting things as they are? What might happen if you do nothing? Some things in our lives we can change and others we can't. We might be able to adjust our behaviour or situation, but sometimes we need to know and accept our limitations. If you cannot change anything, you either have to adjust to live with the problem or try to get out of the situation causing it, but this can be easier said than done. For problems such as abuse, bullying or traumatic reactions, seek help. You might consider leaving or saying 'goodbye' to someone causing the stress. If somebody treats you badly and won't change their attitude or behaviour towards you, 'dump' them and stick with your real friends.

• **Look outside yourself**

Try to find outside interests and, if you can, revive old hobbies or find new ones. Consider joining a club or offer to help with a local charity. Look for help from other resources or people, especially from someone you trust.

• **Look inside yourself**

Take a close look at what you believe about yourself, your life and situation and at the person, thing or circumstances causing the stress.

• Do you have any religious or other basic beliefs, attitudes or assumptions which contribute to the stress? What are these ideas and beliefs? How are they affecting or resulting in the stress and do you need to challenge or change them?
• Can you see any meaning or purpose in what has happened or is happening and what is it telling you about the situation and other people and about you?
• Can you change the way you think and the way you feel! Try 'Reframing' your interpretation or reactions.
• Can you see 'The Cowboy on the Horse', as in Chapter 8, or is life just a meaningless jumble?
• Can you see yourself, other people, things or the incident in a different way?

- **Relax**

This can be one of the most difficult things to do when you are stressed because your whole system can be geared up to continue to react.

- Relaxation techniques: these can be meditation, prayer, yoga, sitting quietly at home, in a park, garden, church or somewhere there is silence and peace.
- Relaxation tapes or CDs are available commercially from the internet, your GP or chemist. While listening to a CD and breathing calmly, relaxation techniques usually entail lying on the floor and, beginning with your toes, you tighten them, hold it, then relax them slowly moving up your body to legs, buttocks, chest, arms, fingers and neck, to your head so that your whole body experiences tension and relaxation.
- Listen to your favourite music using headphones and a personal CD player.
- Have a body massage – if you can afford it.
- Take up some physical exercise – walking, jogging, cycling or a mildly energetic sport and, although this might cause physical stress, it is usually good stress and can help you to relax.

- **Take a break**

You might not be able to afford to do this and stress can stop you from moving away from your familiar and safe surroundings and you might just wish to be alone. Sometimes being on your own can be a positive move towards peace and quiet but it can lead to feelings of rejection and isolation. Try doing something different from your normal routine and life-style: perhaps a short break or holiday. Stop taking work home and try to do something else with your time and, unless it would cause further stress, try switching off your mobile 'phone!

- **Laughter and absurdity**

It has already been said that laughter can help to reduce stress but being stressed is not a joke and humour must not be used all the time; sometimes it can be inappropriate and does not help. But it might relieve tension and enable you to see things in a different way.

- Sit back and think about your situation and difficulties. Is there anything absurd or ridiculous about the incident and its consequences or about the people or person causing the stress? If the stress is a person, try to visualise them in a stupid, vulnerable or ridiculous situation: wearing a silly hat or even sitting on the loo or having sex. This might sound rather childish and inappropriate but it can help you to realise that those who are causing the stress are human and to see things in a slightly different way.

- Listen to or watch some of your favourite films or DVDs, especially comedy. Blackadder and Only Fools and Horses are two of the TV programmes or DVDs which make me laugh and relax. You will have your own. There are many humorous clips on the internet on YouTube. Also, smiling and laughing can help to cause physiological and emotional changes in your brain and body.

- **Plan Ahead**

One problem with stress is that it can disorientate and confuse you so that you feel trapped.

- Try to regain some control over your life. Having some kind of control over what you are thinking and doing can reduce tension and stress and help you to feel more 'in charge' of your life.

- Make preparations and plan well beforehand rather than leaving things to the last moment. Plan ahead, if you can, and never rush to do anything. In order to reduce stress, learn to 'hurry slowly!'

Try to 'do what you are doing' and not doing it just to get to somewhere else. Cherish, celebrate and enjoy the present moment!_

• Swearing

Can you or do you swear? You might have objections to swearing but some find that it can be cathartic and satisfying to shout or swear and it might help to reduce symptoms of stress. It is common for people to scream, swear or shout out loud in frustration and anger when something traumatic, awful, threatening or unjust happens.

A recent TV programme demonstrated that swearing can help to reduce levels of pain. While the presenter timed them, he asked individuals to put one hand into ice-cold water for as long as they could and to keep repeating a fairly ordinary or non-threatening word such as 'lovely'. When the pain became too much they were to remove their hands from the icy water. The experiment was repeated with the same people putting one hand into ice-cold water while repeating a swear-word of their choosing. Swearing helped them to bear the pain for about 50 per cent longer! So, swearing might also help you to cope with stressful events or people, even if you have to do it 'under your breath'! You will probably need to be careful about where, when and with or at whom you swear, but it can be a form of catharsis: it can help to release emotions and feelings. It would also help if you could go into a remote place where you can shout and scream out loud. Into the middle of a wood or field might be a good place to start! You might also shout out loud in your own home when you are on your own.

• Talking

Talking can also help but it should be to the 'right person' at the 'right time', in the 'right place': a safe and confidential situation with someone you trust. Denying there is a problem is generally not helpful but you might not want to talk about it and this should be respected.

Many thousands of people have lived with trauma for years, experiencing the devastating effects that stress, PTS and PTSD has had on their lives, without knowing what was wrong with them or their partners or relatives. They have endured the stress, trauma and pain for decades without any help or support and many have coped by just 'putting up with it'. This applies to civilians, military and ex-military personnel, their partners, families and friends. However, many have looked for help and found that some form of therapy or counselling has helped them to cope and changed their lives.

- Looking for and accepting help

Those who develop reactions of PTS or PTSD can find it extremely difficult to cope and this can have a devastating effect on their families and even on friends or those who work with them. One major problem is that those who suffer from traumatic stress experience symptoms such as depression, shame, guilt and fear of stigma and can be deterred from looking for help; some will deny that there is anything wrong with them. Partners or families will also suffer and have problems in coping and might need help. If you find that you cannot cope or that things are getting difficult, it is no solution to put your head in the sand and continue to suffer. Admit that you have a problem and look for help.

- Arrange to see your GP, priest, chaplain, minister, rabbi, imam or someone known to you. However, you might prefer to talk to someone who doesn't know you. If you work for an organisation or company, speak to someone you can trust such as a welfare officer, chaplain, or someone in occupational health or human resources. These people should treat any contact as confidential and if they can't help they can usually point you to someone who can. Your GP might have a counsellor available in the surgery or can refer you to a psychiatrist, clinical psychologist, therapist, trauma counsellor or clinical hypnotist.

- There are many civilian helping agencies such as Victim Support or the Citizen's Advice Bureaux and their contact telephone numbers will be in the local phone book or on the internet. Some organisations employ a professional counselling agency to help – for free.

- If you have served in the military, even for a very short time, there are a number of specialist charities offering help, support and treatment such as SSAFA and Combat Stress. There are also many local agencies so do look around for them. Some of these are listed in Appendix B but there are many more.

- Do not be put off by the words 'counselling', 'therapy', 'psychologist', 'psychiatrist' or 'psychotherapist'. These professionals should not poke or probe into your personal or private life and background unless it is relevant and helpful. They will not patronise you or treat you as someone who is mad. If they do, find someone else.

- Do not look for miracles or magic wands and accept that counselling or therapy might be painful and difficult but you might be relieved to find that there is someone who understands and can help. You might also discover strengths and resources inside you which you never knew existed!

Appendix B

LOOKING FOR HELP

The following are agencies or charities that offer help to those suffering from the effects of traumatic events. Some specialise in working with ex-service personnel and others offer advice and help to anyone. Where treatment is suggested, contact your GP first to find out whether or not referral via the NHS is possible. All those listed have sites on the internet and contact with them is confidential.

Assist: 11 Albert Street, Rugby, Warwicks, CV21 2RX. Tel: 01788 560 800. Assist is a charity offering confidential, emotional and practical support to individuals and families affected by trauma.

Avon & Wiltshire Mental Health NHS Trust – South West Veteran's Mental Health Service: Tel: 01225 325 689

British Association for Counselling and Psychotherapy: BACP House, 15 St John's Business Park, Lutterworth, Leics. Tel: 01455 883 330.
The BACP have a list of counsellors throughout the UK who specialise in trauma work, some of whom work privately so you would have to pay for therapy.

British Legion – see under 'Royal British Legion'.

The Citizens' Advice Bureau: find the telephone number and address in your local directory. There is one in every city and in most major towns.

Camden and Islington: Veterans' Community: The Traumatic Stress Clinic, 73 Charlotte Street, London W1T 4PL. Tel: 0203 317 6820 or 0203 317 3500.

Cardiff: Community Veterans Mental Health Service, Monmouth House, University Hospital of Wales, Heath Park, Cardiff, CF14 4XW. Tel: 02920 742 062.

Combat Stress: Tyrwhitt House, Oaklawn Road, Leatherhead, Surrey,
KT22 0BX. General enquiries: Tel: 0800 138 1619.

Cornwall: Community Veterans Mental Health Service, Trevillis House, Lodge Hill, Liskeard, Cornwall, PL14 4NE. Tel: 0157 937 3737 or 01208 034 600.

Help for Heroes.   Help for ex-Services' personnel.
Wiltshire: Tel: 01980 844 200.
Catterick: Tel: 01748 834 148.
Colchester: Tel: 01206 818 800.
Plymouth: Tel: 01752 562 179.

Lothian: Rivers Centre. Tel: 0131 451 7400.

Medical Assessment Programme. The Veterans' and Reserves' Mental Health Programme, Chilwell, Nottingham, NG9 5HA. Tel: 0800 169 5401.

National Gulf Veterans' & Families' Association: Tel: 0845 257 4853
This is an independent charity supporting military personnel and their families affected by the two Gulf Wars and Afghanistan.

Royal British Legion: 199 Borough High Street, London SE11AA. Tel: 0203 207 2100
The Royal British Legion works with many other organisations, including 'Help for Heroes', in assisting military personnel who have been wounded, injured or are sick, and their families.

SSAFA (Forces Help): Forcesline: Tel: 0800 731 4880. SSAFA offers life-long help to anyone, and their family, who has served one day or more in the armed forces.

Service Personnel and Veterans Agency. Free help and advice.Helpline: Tel: 0808 191 4218.

South West Veterans Mental Health: see under Avon & Wiltshire Mental Health NHS Trust. Tel: 01225 325 689.

Tees, Esk and Wear Valleys: St Aidan's House, St Aidan's Walk, Bishop Auckland, County Durham, DL14 6SA. Tel: 01325 552 000.

Victim Support: find the telephone number in your local telephone directory. Victim Support Centre in London: Tel: 0808 168 9291.

The UK Trauma Group. Tel: 0797 999 4057, 01787 221 294. This is a group of clinics and units, some of which are privately run, based throughout the UK. You can find them on their website under 'UK Trauma Group' where there are contact addresses, names and telephone numbers. Some are under NHS Trusts and hospitals and a few are private hospitals but all have psychological or psychiatric professional help. They have hospitals in the following towns and cities:

Aberdeen, Belfast, Cambridge, Cardiff, Colchester, Edinburgh, Glasgow, Humberside, Lancashire, Leeds, Lincoln, Lisburn, London (numerous hospitals and agencies), Newcastle, Manchester, Nottingham (the Medical Assessment Programme), Northampton, Nottingham, Northumberland, Oxford, Merseyside, Plymouth, Reading, Swindon, Watford, Witney (Oxfordshire) and York.

There are also many other hospitals and clinics throughout the UK. Contact your GP for information and details of local psychological and psychiatric services and other help. You might need a referral from your GP. If the hospital or clinic is private, sometimes your GP or local NHS Trust will pay, but you will normally have to pay fees, which can be quite high. Do ask about costs.

Appendix C

FURTHER READING

Alexander, Larry, *Biggest Brother*, New American Library, 2005.

Ambrose, Stephen E, *Band of Brothers*, Pocket Books (Simon & Schuster), 2001.

Babington, A., *For the Sake of Example*, London: Paladin, 1985.

Barham, P., *Forgotten Lunatics of the Great War*, Yale University Press, 2004.

Bennett, Glin, *Beyond Endurance*, London: Vintage Secker & Warburg, 1983.

Bettelheim, B., *The Informed Heart*, London: Pelican/Peregrine Books, 1986.

Corns, C., & Hughes-Wilson, J., *Blindfold and Alone*, London: Cassell, 2001.

Dyregrov, A. *Caring for people in disaster situations: psychological Debriefing*. Paper presented at survival seminar, Tavistock Clinic, London, 3 March 1989.

Downing, Taylor, *Breakdown. The Crisis of Shell-shock*, Little Brown, 2016.

Egan, Gerard, *The Skilled Helper*, Belmont, California: Brooks/Cole, 1975.

Finkel, D., *The Good Soldiers*, London: Atlantic Books, 2010.

Gibson, M., *Order from Chaos*, Bristol: BSW Policy Press, 2006.

Goleman, D. *Social Intelligence*, London: Hutchinson, 2006.

Goleman, D., *Emotional Intelligence*, London: Bloomsbury, 1996.

Harig, Paul T., and Sprenger, William D, *Factors of Man-made Stress*, Paper presented at mental health conference, Kuwait, April 1995.

Herbert, C. & Wetmore, A., *Overcoming Traumatic Stress*, London: Robinson, 1999.

Holden, Wendy, *Shell-shock*, Channel 4 Books, London: Macmillan, 1998.

Holmes, R, *Acts of War: the Behaviour of Men in Battle*, London, Cassel Military Paperbacks, 1985.

Janoff-Bulman, R., *Shattered Assumptions*, New York: The Free Press, 1992.

Keegan, John, *The Face of Battle*, London: Pimlico, 1991.

Keenan, B., *An Evil Cradling*, London: Vintage Press, 1992.

Kinchen, D., *Post Traumatic Stress Disorder*, London: Thorsons.

McManners, Hugh, *The Scars of War*, London: Harper Collins, 1994.

Mitchell, J.T., & Everly, G.S., *Critical Incident Stress Debriefing, An Operations Manual*, Elliott City, Maryland, USA: Chevron Publishing, 1995.

Oliver, Neil, *Not Forgotten*, London: Hodder & Stoughton, 2005.

Parkinson F. W., *Coping with Post-Trauma Stress*, London: Sheldon Press, 2000.

Parkinson, F. W., *Critical Incident Debriefing*, London:

Souvenir Press: 1997.

Parkinson, F. W., *Post Trauma Stress*, London: Sheldon Press, 1993 and Fisher Books, USA: Tucson, Arizona, 1993.

Parkinson, F., W., *Listening and Helping in the Workplace*, London: Sheldon Press, 2005.

Pincus, Lily, *Death & the Family*, London: Faber & Faber, 1997.

Putkowski, J and & Sykes, *Shot at Dawn*, London: Pen & Sword, 1993.

Regel, S, & Joseph, S, *Post-Traumatic-Stress*, Oxford University Press, 2010.

Rowe, Dorothy. *Beyond Fear*, London: Fontana, 1987.

Saari, Salli, *A Bolt from the Blue*, London: Jessica Kingsley Publications, 2005.

Scott, M. J, and Stradling, S., G., *Counselling for Post Traumatic Stress Disorder*, London: Sage Publications, 1992.

Scott, M. J., & Stradling, S.,G,. *Trauma & Post-Traumatic-Stress Disorder, London*: Cassell, 2000.

Shapiro, F., E.M.D.R., *Basic Principles*, Guildford Press, 2001.

Shepherd, Ben, *A War of Nerves*, London: Jonathan Cape, 2000.

Shepherd, Ben, *Headhunters*, The Bodley Head, 2014.

Tedeschi & Calhoun, *Trauma & Transformation*, London: Sage, 1995.

Turnbull, G, Dr/Professor, *Trauma*, London: Bantam Press, 2011

Turner, B., & Rennell, T., *When Daddy Came Home*, B.C.A., 1995.

van der Kolk editor et al, *Traumatic Stress*, Guildford Press, 1996.

Weekes, Claire, *Peace from Nervous Suffering*, London: Angus & Robertson, 1972.

Winters, Major Dick, *Beyond Band of Brothers*, Ebury Press, 2001.

Wolpert, Lewis, *Malignant Sadness*, London: Faber & Faber, 1999.

Index